How To Design And Deliver Great Training

Learn how to turn any material into lively, engaging and effective training

by

Alan Matthews

First published 2012

www.hlspublishing.com

ISBN-13: 978-1480216280e

Copyright © Alan Matthews

Acknowledgements

My thanks to all the following who have given their time by reviewing drafts of the book, making helpful suggestions and spotting the inevitable typos and errors:

Marek Tribedi, Paul Roper, Sheina Rigg, Susan Pullen, Lyn Hartman, Jeffrey Kirn, Wendy Thistle, Colin Bates, Carol Stevenson, Anne Robert, Maureen Lobatto, Gary Bedingfield, Geoffrey Seaman, Robert M. Ring, Jane Smith, Manuela Wedgwood, Sue Haswell, Felicity Morath, Kym Kirk, Alison Reeves, Deborah Swarts, Alan Sweeney, Heather Sheen, Samuel Wepener, Ruth McGrath, Tammy Harper.

Thanks also to all the trainers I have ever worked with, all of whom I have learned from and most of whom have been amazingly generous with their support and ideas. Some of them will have contributed to this book without them, or me, realising it (I honestly can't remember where I first came across some of the activities I've mentioned and the trainers who passed them on to me probably got them from someone else in the first place).

And, most of all, thanks to my wife, Catherine, without whom none of this would be possible or even worthwhile.

What people are saying about this book

"*This book is excellent, I wish it had been around years ago when I first took training sessions...a nice balance between the theory and the practical.*"

Sue Pullen

"*I absolutely adore your book! Just going through the book has helped me tremendously. I found the format perfect for reading. I have been training now for 12 years and this is the most readable book I have come across.*"

Tammy Harper

"*...an easy, fun and informative read – not just for people who are new to training but also for those who have been involved for a number of years. This book is a valuable resource for anyone who wants to continue to develop their training practice, I thoroughly recommend it.*"

Jane Smith

"*I really did find this book very useful and informative. It is good to have a book written in layman's terms and it left me with the impression that it was written just for me. It has given me ideas on how I can improve my training and make each session more interactive and memorable.*"

Paul Roper

"*...this book turned out to be a rare gem of a training tool. Alan's joy for training is infectious and shines through every page. With his own down-to-earth style, he uses real-life scenarios to provide valuable* examples throughout. The only thing stopping this becoming a 'training textbook' is that it's so much fun!"

Sue Haswell

"...a comprehensive guide that will definitely provide a great roadmap for new trainers. I found it a very easy read with realistic examples and concepts that can be used in real life situations."

Wendy Thistle

"If you only read one book on workplace learning, this book should be at the top of your list...perfectly suited for the new trainer who is tasked to design in-house training programmes, develop relevant content and deliver training, all to a professional standard."

Kym Kirk

"...a clear and focused roadmap for the new facilitator, while also serving as a valuable resource for those experienced trainers who are looking for new approaches."

Jeffrey Kirn

"...excellent, chatty and practical book, full of techniques, tips and reminders to deliver transformational training, emphasising the steps to become the all-important facilitative and creative trainer. I found it an enjoyable read and a good reference book without jargon, which I'm sure both newer and experienced trainers will dip into often for inspiration and good practice."

Maureen Lobatto

"Alan has come up with a 'must-have' book for all trainers, both new and experienced. He covers all aspects of the training process – his book is a great learning tool for new trainers or those who don't train very often, but also serves as a great reminder to those who have been training for some time. I thoroughly recommend it to anyone involved in training."

Alison Reeves

"I found this book very informative, easy to read, containing learning for everyone involved in training, whether they are just starting out or have been trainers for some time."

Heather Sheen

"I think it's an excellent book - a great read with many, many interesting and useful tips. I have been training for 15 years and I still got plenty from the book."

Felicity Morath

"I found this to be a great reference for both the trainer just starting out and the experienced trainer."

Robert M Ring

"...excellent for new trainers or experienced trainers who want to dip in and out of the chapters...I have been training for years and it was good to have reinforcement that what I am doing is pretty good but also reminded me of some areas I need to revisit."

Carol Stevenson

"...a comprehensive, clear and simple guide to training issues. It focussed throughout on good practice, used humour appropriately and above all was very clear and straightforward."

Geoffrey Seaman

Contents

Acknowledgements   4

What people are saying about this book   5

Why Should You Read This Book?   9

Chapter 1: How People Learn   19

Chapter 2: How To Design Your Training   47

Chapter 3: How To Get People In The Mood For Learning   79

Chapter 4: How To Use Questions To Promote Learning   108

Chapter 5: How To Choose And Use Activities   133

Chapter 6: How To Use Visual Aids   165

Chapter 7: How To Help People Remember   193

Chapter 8: How To Deliver With Impact   218

Chapter 9: How To Set Up The Room   234

Chapter 10: How To Handle Difficult Behaviour   248

Chapter 11: How To Evaluate Training   266

What Will You Do Next?   282

Appendix 1 - Resources you may need for a training session   284

Appendix 2 - 10 things to send people before a training course   288

How Can I Help You?   290

References   292

Who Is Alan Matthews?   293

Bonus Materials: There are some free materials available to supplement what you have learned in this book. To claim your bonuses, go to www.transformyourtraining.com/book-bonuses

Why Should You Read This Book?

Who is this book for?

To put it very simply, this book is for anyone who wants to design and deliver training which is exciting, engaging and enjoyable.

It will help you to take basic information or content, however dull or complex it might seem, and turn it into memorable and effective learning material.

Whether you're a full time trainer already or someone who does a bit of training as part of another job, applying what you learn here will put you way ahead of the great majority of trainers out there.

Why? Because it's based on:

- sound learning theory and proven training practice

- over 20 years experience of day to day involvement in designing and delivering training, both in skills and in complex technical subjects

- over 20 years of research into learning and development

- over 20 years of working with a great variety of other trainers and copying their best ideas (don't worry, they know - and we all do it).

Oh, and about 18 years experience in running Train the Trainer courses and working with hundreds of trainers, hearing their questions and their concerns and helping them develop their skills and confidence.

The techniques in this book WORK, simple as that.

This book will help you if you are:

- a full time trainer in an organisation

- a line manager who has to pass on skills and knowledge to others

- an IT specialist who has to train others to use software

- a technical expert who has to explain complex ideas or processes to others

- an independent training professional

Of course, just reading the manual won't do anything by itself. You have to try out the ideas in it and practice them as you would any other skill.

But the techniques and tips you read here can equip you to deliver training which is both memorable and fun, whatever the topic or the group you are training.

What will you get from this book?

I would hazard a guess that you first came into training because you were really good at something else.

Maybe you had some specific technical knowledge or skills and, at some point, you were asked to pass these on to others.

That's how I first got involved in training myself, I was a Tax Consultant and I was asked to help deliver some Tax courses for other people in the firm I worked for.

Over time, you may well have come to find that you enjoy training and you have developed a way of doing it which usually works reasonably well for you. You have picked up ideas from other people you've seen training or it may just be your own natural style.

The problem is, if you don't have a grounding in the theory and practice of training, it tends to be a process of trial and error. It takes a long time to develop a successful approach.

And your range of choices may be limited. You know that some things seem to work, but you don't know exactly why. You find that some approaches don't work so well in some situations, but you don't know what else to try.

This book will help you to shortcut that learning.
It will give you:

- a broad range of tools to use

- the knowledge and understanding to be flexible in your approach as a trainer

- the confidence and judgement to choose the right approach in the right situation.

You will learn:

- how people learn and remember

- how to design, deliver and evaluate training

- how to select the right content for any group

- how to make your training interactive and interesting

- how to deal with " difficult " behaviour

- how to get a good response from the grumpiest, most reluctant learners

Are you a good presenter? Sorry, that's not enough!

There's a message repeated throughout this book that training should be interactive and participative. In other words, if you want to be an effective trainer, you're not just a presenter. You don't just deliver information to a passive, silent "audience".

That's not to say that good presentation skills aren't important. They are. Part of your role will be to put information across to people, to get their attention, to make complex ideas sound simple – all the skills of a good presenter will be necessary.

But it's not enough.

However good you might be at giving presentations, that in itself will not make you the outstanding trainer you want to be.

Why? Because people don't learn effectively by listening to presentations, even really good ones. The early parts of the manual will explain why that is. It's to do with how the brain works and how adults learn.

So, if you're a great presenter, that's a good start, but you'll have to change some habits to make the transformation into a facilitative trainer.

What does "facilitative trainer" mean?

Well, it means you see your role as structuring an environment which allows people to learn what they need to learn. You design (and facilitate) activities, exercises and discussions which will lead to successful learning taking place.

That suggests:

- using a variety of approaches and styles

- varying your methods to suit the group and the topic you're working with

- encouraging involvement and participation.

To be an outstanding trainer, you will:

- see your role as drawing out, and building on, people's existing knowledge rather than pouring information into people's brains as if they are empty vessels needing to be filled up

- make sure that the learners are active and involved all the time

- not see yourself as the only person in the room with valuable knowledge or something to contribute

- make sure that what is taught is relevant and practical and related to real situations so that learners can apply it easily

- let the learners talk more than you do

- design training which allows for a variety of learning styles and preferences

If that sounds a tall order, don't worry, the book will show you exactly how to do this.

Is classroom based training out of date?

The training I'm talking about in this book could largely be called "classroom- based", which means it involves getting a number of live human beings together in a room for a certain length of time.

However, there are many other ways to train people, including one-to-one coaching, webinars and tele-classes and self-study programmes for people to work through by themselves.

When it comes to my own learning, I often use web-based methods, self-study materials with DVDs and mp3s or even good, old-fashioned books rather than attending courses, seminars and workshops.

There are lots of ways in which people can learn, of course, and they all have their place. But, with all this variety of methods, especially with web-based approaches, you may hear the view that classroom-based training has had its day, that it's old-fashioned and ineffective.

Is this true?

No.

Thank you, glad we cleared that up. Next - is there still a place for pencils in the modern office?

If you insist, I'll elaborate a little.

Based on what we know about the brain (and I'll go into more detail later) what are some of the things which seem to help people to learn effectively?

These would include:

- a chance to interact with other people as they learn

- a chance to contribute to, and process, the information they receive

- an opportunity to create meaning rather than just consume information

- physical movement and activity

- variety of approaches and stimuli

- engaging as many senses as possible while learning and the material having an impact at an emotional level as well as an intellectual one

- having controlled repetition and reinforcement

- learning being fun or, at least, an enjoyable experience

- being able to practise and apply skills as they are learned

I would say that well-designed and delivered classroom-based training can tick all of these boxes where no other form of learning can.

It also allows people to share their knowledge and insights, to get away from the workplace for a while to focus on their learning and to get great value from participating in a shared experience with other people.

So mention that to anyone who tells you that your training courses can be replaced by e-learning programmes.

How to make the most of this book
The aim of this book is to promote learning. I want you to learn what you need to be an outstanding trainer. Of course, what that involves will depend on where you are now.

You may be very new to training and nearly everything in this book may be new to you. Or you may be quite an experienced trainer who is reading this because, like all good trainers, you're always on the lookout for another idea. In that case, you may have come across some of this information before.

It doesn't matter what your starting point is, I'm confident you will get nothing of value from this book – unless you take some action afterwards. As with all training, it's what happens next that's important. It's what you do with the information you find here that matters.

You might read the book from start to finish. You may find that, once you get started, you can't put it down.

You might just dip into certain sessions which cover the topics you're most interested in.

You might just sneak a look at the last page to see how it ends. It's up to you.

However you read it, make a note of anything which stands out and do something about it. Don't just think, "Yes, that's a good point. I must remember that." If you see something which is particularly important, highlight it or write it down and then decide what you are going to do to implement it.

And don't try to put everything into practice at once. Pick something which you think is of most value and try it out. Do one thing which makes a difference. Then do another one.

You'll never stop learning. You'll go on developing your skills and your knowledge about training. Work with as many other trainers as you can, watch what they do, learn from both good and bad. That's how you keep moving forward. If this book helps you on that journey, I'll be delighted.

Chapter 1: How People Learn

If you're a trainer, your role is to help people learn. To do that, you need to have some understanding of *how* people learn so that you can give yourself the best chance of success – otherwise, it's going to be hit and miss. You'll find that some things work and some don't but you won't be sure why.

In recent years, some people have started talking about "brain friendly" training, which really just means training based on what we know about how the brain works, how people take in information and how they remember. It seems obvious but, if you can tailor your training to suit the way people learn, isn't that going to make your training more effective?

One difficulty is that our understanding of these things is still developing, and very rapidly. There are lots of different theories and approaches and there's a huge amount of information out there which you could spend a lot of time going through.

I have to admit, I'm fascinated by the whole area of learning and the brain but, for the purposes of this book, I'm going to assume that you are not. You're a busy person, training may only be part of what you do and you really just want an overview to help you understand why certain training methods are more effective than others.

So that's what I'm going to give you. Bear in mind that this is my own interpretation and opinion. If you want to go back to some of the reference material to make up your own mind, there's a list at the end of the book so, if you do want to go into more depth, you can.

There are several ways to approach this:

1. Looking at how the brain works

2. Looking at the process people go through, the stages involved in learning

3. Looking at how people prefer to approach situations where they have to learn something

Here are some ideas which form the basis of most training these days. These will illustrate why I recommend certain approaches, in particular why a presentation or lecture style isn't the most effective form of training and why you should build interaction and activity into your sessions.

How the brain works

Here are some general points about what happens when people are learning. (There'll be more information specifically about memory in the chapter on how to help people remember.)

We look for meaning

The brain can't help but try to impose meaning and order on new information. What do you think this is?

Your brain is working through what it might be but you don't have much information to go on at the moment.

Let me add something. What do you think it is now?

And what about now?

Do you see part of a dog's face? (I'll bet you do now that I've mentioned it).

In fact, these are just shapes on a page. They don't necessarily signify anything at all, but your brain won't accept that. It tries to see some significance in them.

We do the same with written material. Read this sentence.

"Jim was shippling slowly down the street. He tightened his bajoma because the weather was crockling."

I've included some made up words but I'm sure you can still make some sense of it. Although you haven't come across those words before, you try to give them meaning, partly by looking at the context and partly by comparing them to words which you have met before.

If you see something which, at first, doesn't make much sense, there will be a period of confusion while your brain goes to work on it. As a trainer, you can use this but you need to be careful.

Up to a point, this can be helpful. You can make people think by presenting them with something which they have to work out. This can lead people to be curious and to pay attention to what's in front of them. They try to make sense of it and to determine what it means. For some, this will be an interesting challenge.

But for others, and for everyone if it gets too difficult, this may just be baffling. They may give up if they can't understand the information.

If you present them with material which confuses them, they'll waste time and effort trying to impose some order onto it. Save them the trouble by making sure your material is presented logically and by setting out the context for them, i.e. give them the "big picture" before going into the finer details of a topic.

We connect new information with existing knowledge

That's what your brain did when it tried to make sense of the shapes and the made up words. It compared them with everything it knew which had some similarity to them.

You can help people learn by making connections clear to them, by pointing out similarities or differences between what they already know and what you want them to learn.

Relate new information to things people are already familiar with. Use stories which they can relate to when you introduce new material.

For example, when I used to train people in Tax I would talk to them about situations they had met before rather than diving straight into complex legislation.

If I was talking about Capital Gains Tax, which is based on the profit you make when you sell certain assets, I would start by talking about the sort of things you might own which would be worth something if you sold them. People would suggest cars, houses, shares, paintings, jewellery.

These are all examples of assets and they are all things which people have come across before.

Similarly Tax, like many other subjects, has its own vocabulary. For example, in Inheritance Tax there were things called dispositions. What does this mean? In most cases it means a gift. People know what gifts are, so I would start by talking about those and then move on to any other examples of dispositions.

So I was starting from the familiar before moving on to new information. This helps people to put the new ideas into context and to feel that they already have some useful knowledge about the subject.

We learn actively, not passively

Another example of what just happened when you looked at the drawings and the sentence. The brain processes information, it does something with it. It is not a blank canvas or an empty bucket waiting to be filled up with knowledge. As I mentioned above, it interacts with information in order to make sense of it and to make connections with existing knowledge.

Even on an unconscious level, people will have questions about anything they learn. As soon as they hear a piece of information, they'll think, "What does this mean? What can I do with this information? What difference does this make? How does it fit in with everything else I know?"

You can ask learners these questions yourself to help them to process what they have learned. When you introduce some new idea, ask them, "So what does that mean for you in practice? How can you use this information?"

People learn and remember more effectively when they're given an opportunity to do this processing, to discuss ideas, to talk about things, to reflect, to apply what they have learned.

This is one reason why lecturing is not very effective. The audience have little chance to engage with the information, they are just passive.

I can remember sitting in lectures taking huge amounts of notes when I was at college. Some time later, I'd look back at the notes and I couldn't remember even taking them, never mind what they were meant to be about. This is typical of lectures or presentations. Very little sticks because the brain isn't allowed to do what it needs to do – interact with the information.

We learn by conscious and unconscious processing

I mentioned processing earlier. This can take place through discussion with others, through personal reflection, through applying what has been learned. But it can also take place unconsciously.

Sleep has been shown to be an important part of learning. Your unconscious brain processes information and also works on problems while you sleep – have you ever woken up during the night with a head full of ideas or with the answer to some problem that you've been thinking about?

Your unconscious brain has continued processing the problem while you were asleep.

This doesn't mean that you should let people have a nap when you're training but it does show the importance of regular breaks.

Breaks are also important because the part of the brain which takes in new information can be overloaded (I'm sure you know the feeling). Learners can get to a point where they just can't take in any more and they need to do something else while their brain gets to work on what they have learned.

We look for answers to questions

We tend to notice, and remember, information which answers a question we have had in our minds.

Have you ever sat waiting at the doctor's or the dentist's and picked up a magazine? You may have browsed through it and glanced at a couple of articles. Unless something particularly stood out as being relevant or useful to you, you probably wouldn't remember much of what you read. Your brain hardly engages with it at all and makes no attempt to store it in the memory.

But think about times when you've had a particular question in your mind and you're looking for specific information to answer that question. Then you pay more attention, you pick out key information and you remember it much more effectively.

As a trainer you can use this to help people to learn by preparing them beforehand – pose questions, get them to think about what they need to learn and how it will help them. Build curiosity and interest so that, when your learners come across the material you are giving them, they are primed to look for answers and to remember what they learn.

We learn by using all our senses

Memory is strengthened if information is supported by strong sensory (and emotional) connections. The more senses involved in taking in information, the stronger the retention.

Memory can also be tied to sensory associations, for example there are probably some smells which make you instantly recall some scene from your childhood – maybe the smell of certain foods cooking, of cut grass, of rain on tarmac (that makes me remember the school playground). It's the strong association with the senses, and often the emotional connection, which makes the memory so powerful.

This is why you should support learning through verbal, visual, auditory and other stimuli. Later chapters will show you how to do that.

What does this mean for you as a trainer?

All this supports the idea of learning being an active, or interactive, process. It's not passive, it's not a question of the trainer feeding people information which they just absorb. Effective learning involves:

- activity

- a search for meaning and understanding

- an opportunity to process and

- an engagement between the trainer, the learner and the material.

The Kolb Learning Cycle

This is a very popular model of learning which is used by many trainers as a basis for designing their training sessions. It has also been used as a way of determining people's learning styles or preferences, which I'll come on to later.

Like virtually all models of learning, this has its critics. You would be hard pressed to find any theory or model which was universally accepted. However, I like it because:

- it seems to me to suit most, if not all, learning situations

- it accords with my own experience and

- it seems to offer a useful illustration of the stages people have to go through in order to learn effectively, which you can use as a simple template when designing your training.

Warning – again, this is my interpretation of Kolb's model. I'd recommend you go back to the original at some point, particularly if you want to refer to the model yourself in your training.

I say this because many trainers (myself included) have made the mistake of referring to theories or models which they haven't actually read themselves, they've only read or heard other people's accounts of them.

So one person gives a summary of a theory, another picks it up and slightly changes it, someone else hears that and repeats it…until the end result is a gross oversimplification or misrepresentation of the original work.

Having said that, here goes.

David Kolb published his model in 1984.

The model suggests four stages which all learners must go through to learn most effectively (and I'm using my own labels here for the four stages, you may come across slightly different ones in other accounts).

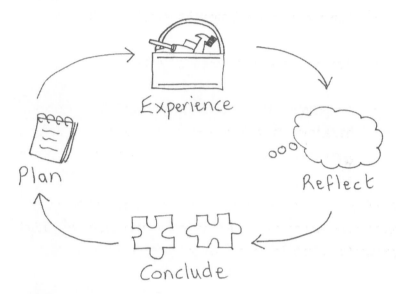

Experience – you do something. For example, you give a presentation, you have a meeting with a client, you try to do a calculation or to use some software or a piece of equipment.

Reflect – you think about what happened – what was the result, what worked, what didn't work?

Conclude – you draw conclusions, you generalise about what you have seen and thought about. At this stage you might ask, "Why?" Why did some things work and others not?

Also, at this stage, you make connections – you see that there are trends in how you approach things. You may also seek further information - you read manuals, you talk to people, you do some research.

Plan – you prepare to have another go. You plan to keep the things which seem to work well and perhaps to change some of the things which don't, you try some new approaches based on what you learned from the first attempt, you experiment.

Let's take the example of being a trainer.
You're asked to deliver a training session.

- You have a go (experience).

- Then, afterwards, you think about how it went (reflect) – you see that some things were successful, some less so.

- You might then talk to other trainers about how they do things, you read a manual, you watch people, you start to see some patterns in terms of what works and what doesn't (conclude).

- Having picked up some more information you prepare another session, adapting your approach (plan).

As I mentioned, you can start anywhere on the cycle. In fact, if you were asked to deliver a training session, it's unlikely you would just walk in and start without any thought beforehand. You might:

- think about training sessions you had run before, or at least seen (reflect)

- you would get some more ideas, perhaps from manuals or other people so you could form some general ideas about what effective training would be like (conclude) and then

- prepare your session (plan) before

- delivering the session (experience)

So your cycle might then be – reflect, conclude, plan, experience. Then, after the session, you would start to think about what happened and so go round again.

You adapt your approach as you go along, learning and improving all the time.

As a model, I think this has a number of advantages:

1. It makes sense, i.e. it does seem to describe the way people learn in all sorts of situations, although it's particularly relevant where people are learning skills.

2. It's simple.

3. It's very useful as a basis for designing and reviewing training – you can easily look at any training you've planned and see whether it covers the whole learning cycle.

For instance, if you're designing a session on dealing with customers, you might start with an activity where people practice handling a difficult customer.

But that's not enough in itself – how will people learn from it? You need to allow time for them to reflect on what happened, discuss it, get feedback, consider some ideas and then think about what it means, how it affects the way they work and what they would do differently next time.

Alternatively, you could start by discussing some ideas about dealing with customers and ask how people feel about it. You could discuss people's experiences and some problems they've encountered. They could share strategies and tips.

Then you might introduce an exercise where they have some time to plan and work together before practising their skills.

After the activity, you would lead a debrief - a discussion and feedback session - to take them through the cycle again.

In both cases, you've taken people through the cycle, you've just started from different points.

Learning Styles

If you want to learn about something, what's the first thing you do?

I know what I do. I buy books.

I read as much as I can about a subject. And I think about it a lot.

Then I like to talk to other people about the ideas I've come across. I like a good discussion, it helps me to think things through.

Is that what you would do? There's a good chance that it is not. For some people the least effective (and least interesting) way for them to try to learn something would be to read a book about it.

Another example – if I want to drive somewhere, I look at a map and I can hold in my mind a pretty good impression of where I need to go. On the other hand, if someone gives me some directions, e.g. "Go second left, first right, then take the A241...", I forget them instantly.

However, friends of mine can remember directions much more easily but can't read or remember a map.

You see, people have different ways of learning. Although our brains are the same in most respects, we have different preferences about the ways we take in and process new information.

For example, some people prefer to read, others to listen, others to watch videos, others to simply have a go at something.

Some people like to be active, others like time to reflect and consider things.

Some need other people around them, to discuss ideas with, to challenge them and make them think. Others prefer to be by themselves and to think on their own.

Some people need to know the theory behind things, others just want to know what works.

The key point is that people are different. Not everyone will want to learn things the same way that you do.

There are many different models of learning styles, looking at learning from various angles and, as I mentioned earlier, all these theories and models have their critics.

For example, some theories of learning styles suggest that:

- people can be categorised according to their learning styles, e.g. they are "visual" learners or "kinaesthetic" learners

- these styles can be accurately identified by means of some instrument, e.g. a questionnaire

- the most effective way of training would be to find out a person's learning style and present all information in that style because that would be how the person would prefer to learn, regardless of the subject matter

This may be going too far. It suggests that some people can only learn in a certain way. In fact, we all learn in a variety of ways, using all our senses, and we may vary our approach depending on the subject matter we are learning. We all take in information visually and aurally, for example, and we all share the general characteristics of the brain that I set out earlier.

Having said that, I do think people can have quite strong preferences about the way they approach learning situations - perhaps influenced by past experience, upbringing, education, habit, general interests or just the way their brains happen to be wired.

As a trainer, I think it's very helpful to remember that not everyone approaches learning in the same way and that, if you're designing training, you need to bear in mind that other people may not share your favoured approach.

If you only present information in one way, you are restricting everyone's access to it and limiting their ability to learn it. The key is variety.

I don't propose to go through the various models here but I do want to mention two. I have chosen these, not because there is more scientific evidence to support them but because they do appear to me to accord with the experience of most trainers.

In other words, they do illustrate some of the common differences trainers find in the people they work with. Also, I think both are helpful when you're trying to design training which will have the best chance of engaging all your learners.

Honey and Mumford's model

I include this model partly because it's a very popular one which you will almost certainly come across and, in my opinion, very helpful as a general guide when you're preparing training.

Honey and Mumford built a model of learning styles around Kolb's learning cycle.

They found that people sometimes have a strong preference for one of the stages in the cycle. Again, I would warn against trying to put people firmly into one or other boxes – we all learn using all these elements. So, when I'm describing "types" here, these are extreme examples to illustrate the model.

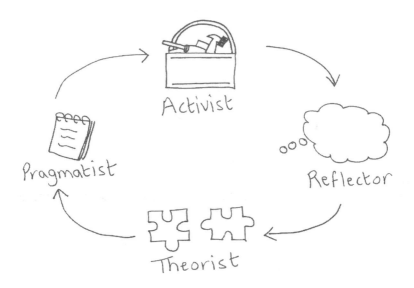

Activists

Activists prefer the Experience stage of the cycle.

They enjoy doing things rather than talking about them. They prefer the activity itself to the planning or debriefing stages.

On a training course, Activists will be the ones who enjoy getting into small groups and building things or getting their hands on some equipment. But they'll be drumming their fingers if the discussion session goes on too long.

If they buy a new DVD player or camera, they won't spend time reading the manual, they'll press the buttons and find out how it works by playing with it. If they buy a flat – pack wardrobe, they'll discard the instructions and just put it together (when I mentioned this on a course once, a woman said, "That explains my husband!")

Activists are quite happy to make mistakes, they learn from them.

Activists are happy when:

- given new experiences and challenges

- working with others in team activities

- being thrown in the deep end without too much time to prepare

- involved in fast – moving sessions with variety

Activists are less happy when:

- listening to lectures or long explanations

- given too much time to reflect on their own

- asked to absorb a lot of data

- debriefing activities or listening to feedback

- discussing theoretical models or ideas

Reflectors

Reflectors like the Reflect stage of the cycle (not surprisingly).

They like to research, consider and plan before taking any action. They like to listen to discussions but also to spend time by themselves thinking and processing information.

They won't like situations where they're rushed from one activity to the next.

They prefer to take their time and they don't like to make mistakes.

Reflectors are happy when:

- discussing ideas

- reviewing what has happened and thinking about what they've learned

- given plenty of time to prepare for tasks

- working by themselves

Reflectors are less happy when:

- asked to do things with no time to prepare

- experiencing things which are unfamiliar

- moving from one activity after another with no time to consider what has happened

- working under pressure or to tight deadlines

Theorists

Theorists like the Conclude stage of the cycle.

They like to generalise and make connections between ideas. They like to discuss models and theories. They think problems through step – by – step and don't take action without planning it out first.

A Theorist who bought a DVD player or camera would read the manual, probably from start to finish. If they bought a self-assembly wardrobe, they would read the instructions and set out all the pieces before they tried to put it together.

Theorists are happy when:

- put in complex situations where they have to apply their knowledge

- they understand the reason for any activity they're asked to carry out

- they can discuss concepts, ideas and theories

- they have the chance to question and challenge ideas

Theorists are less happy when:

- they can see no clear purpose to an activity

- they have to do things without knowing the principles involved

- they're given isolated tasks to do with no apparent connection or link to the learning

Pragmatists

Pragmatists like the Plan stage of the cycle.

They like relevance, they like to know what works. They'll listen to ideas if they are practical but may get impatient if there's a lot of discussion of theories which they see as too abstract. They like to try things out in practice and to get involved in activities.

Pragmatists reading this book might not bother reading this chapter. Instead they would look for a chapter which said, "The 10 top tips for..." or "How to...". If they bought a piece of equipment, they might read the "Quick Start" booklet so they could get it working, but they wouldn't bother with the rest.

Pragmatists are happy when:

- they can see how to apply what they're learning

- they have the chance to try out techniques

- they can see the relevance and benefit of a topic

- they are given a model or process which they can put into practice

Pragmatists are less happy when:

- they can see no obvious or immediate benefit to what they're learning

- there's no guidance on how to apply what they've learned

- the event or learning is 'all theory'

Dunn and Dunn's Model

Rita and Kenneth Dunn set out 5 "dimensions" in which people's learning styles may differ:

Environmental:

Some people prefer quiet, some noise. (I prefer to work in silence but I know people who can't concentrate unless there's a radio on in the background.) Some people prefer formal or informal surroundings.

Emotional:

Some people need a lot of support and guidance, others like to be left alone to work things out for themselves. Some people are more motivated than others, some have more persistence.

Sociological:

Some people prefer to work alone, some prefer to work in groups. Some like to have an authority figure to guide them.

Physiological:

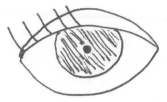

Some people take in information more effectively through visual stimuli, some aurally, some need to move around and be active.

Psychological:

Some people look at the big picture, others go for detail, some are more impulsive, others need more time for reflection.

This seems to be to be a useful summary of the ways in which learners can differ in their preferences. The question is then, what is the trainer meant to do about this? Should you try to cover all the elements, should you accept that learners have preferences and try to cater for them all or should you try to encourage people to adopt other strategies for learning?

What this means for you

I think the main thing to remember from all this is simply that people are different. They have different styles and preferences, perhaps very strong preferences, for particular forms of learning.

Having said that, everyone needs to go through the learning cycle, whichever stage they have a preference for. Not even the keenest Activist learns successfully just by "doing", nor the most avid Theorist just by reading.

Similarly, everyone learns through more than one approach. No – one has just one learning style, we all tend to have a combination. So what does this mean for you as a trainer?

- Your training should include all stages of the learning cycle where possible. Whether you're delivering training to a group in a classroom or working one – to – one, design your training to include a variety of activities, in some ways including experience, reflection, introducing new ideas and planning.

- Whichever stage of the learning cycle you're on (e.g. the activity part or the analysis part) there may well be someone in the group who doesn't like this bit. If you explain why you're doing certain things, this will help to keep the interest of people who might otherwise switch off, as will changing the activity regularly.

- Don't assume that everyone likes to learn the same way you do. When you design a session, you'll probably tend to make it the sort of session you would enjoy yourself but this may not suit someone with a very different learning preference.

Beware of spending too long on the areas which you find most interesting – e.g. explaining some theory in great depth and detail because that's what you would like if you were on the course.

- Allow time for people to work together in pairs and small groups, but also to work alone and reflect by themselves.

- Whether you're working with a group or an individual, use a range of stimuli and media to convey information – verbal presentation, discussion, visual aids, diagrams, illustrations, practical activity, "hands – on" experience, movement and individual reflection.

Again, the first way you think of expressing an idea will probably reflect your own preferred style. Once you've done that, think, "How else can I put this across to suit people who don't learn the same way I do?"

If you're training an individual and that person just doesn't seem to be "getting it", it could be that he or she has a different learning style to you and needs a different approach. Vary your style to find one that works for that person.

The later chapters of this book will help you to design and deliver training which does these things. But, for the moment, you'll see from this chapter just why the presentation or lecture style approach is ineffective and why you need to build variety, activity and interaction into all training events.

Chapter 2: How To Design Your Training

Where do you start?

You've been asked to deliver a training session on some topic, what do you do next? How do you decide what to include, how to put it all together, how to get your points across? This chapter will help you find the answers.

There are 3 main questions you need to ask yourself if you're thinking about designing training:

- Why?

- What?

- How?

Why – why is the training needed? What is it meant to achieve? What's the purpose of it? Who is it for?

What – what content do you need to make sure the training achieves what it's intended to?

How – what methods are most appropriate for delivering the training?

This chapter will help you to determine all three and later sessions will go into more detail on the How.

How to choose your content

A major problem with many training courses or sessions is that they're overloaded with content. This is often because the trainer hasn't done the job of selecting just the content which is needed but has thrown in all sorts of material in the hope that some of it will stick and that people will get something from it.

The trainer's job is to make decisions about exactly what content needs to be included and then to ruthlessly cut out everything else.

To do this, you need to ask two questions:

1. Who is this training for and why do they need it?

2. What do I want them to think, feel and do at the end of it?

1. Who is the training for?

In terms of why people need this training, you need to know as much as possible about the people involved. Before you can determine the content of a course or a session, you need to know about the people you're training and their specific needs. At the very least you need to know:

- who they are

- why they need this training at this moment

- what they're expecting or hoping to get from the course

- what they already know about the topic, what existing background or experience they have in this area

- what previous training they've had

- what they'll want/need/be expected to do with what they've learned after the course

- how they're likely to feel about the course

You may also need to know other factors, such as age, gender, role, level in an organisation, depending on the nature of the training.

It's also useful to know whether people have volunteered to come on the course or whether they've been sent. This can make a great difference to their attitude.

2. Think, feel and do

Remember, at the start, I said you needed to decide what you want the learners to think, feel and do at the end of the training.

Many trainers and designers would express this differently. They might see training as influencing what people "know and do". That's not quite the same thing.

What's important at the end of any training is not just what knowledge people have gained, in terms of what new information they have acquired.

What matters even more is what they think about this information and how they feel about it.

Firstly, people need to have the right attitude to learn something in the first place, they need to be receptive to it and see the benefit of it.

Then they need to have a positive attitude towards implementing what they've learned. If they don't, then nothing will change.

Let's say you're training people in some new regulations which apply to their work. That would be increasing their knowledge.

But what are they going to do with that, how will they use it?

Applying what they've learned will mean changing the way they work. And, after all, if they aren't going to apply it, what's the point of learning it? In this example, they'll need to work in a different way to take account of the new regulations.

Even if they left the course able to recite the new rules or write them out or know where to find them, what would be the point if they were thinking, "Well, I know the new rules but I don't care. I'm going to stick to my old ways of doing things"? What would you have achieved?

Another example is a customer service course. You're training people in ways to keep their customers happy. You can help them to learn all sorts of techniques and give them lots of information but, if they don't have an attitude of wanting to deliver good customer service, all that will be wasted.

So, in designing training, you need to plan both:

- objectives and

- outcomes

Learning objectives

The learning objectives for a course cover what you want people to be able to do at the end of it.

You should write out the learning objectives for any course and for each session within a course.

Why? Because unless you're clear about the ultimate objectives of the course, you can't be as ruthless as you need to be with the content. If you're struggling to make decisions about what to leave in and what to take out, it's usually because you're not clear enough yet about the objectives of the training.

The learning objectives will relate back to the training needs which were identified in the first place. Why do people need training? What needs do they have (or does the organisation have)? What is the training meant to achieve?

Objectives are usually written in behavioural terms, i.e. what will the participants be able to do as a result of the training?

For example:

- Operate a piece of machinery safely and effectively

- Follow a process or set of procedures

- Use some software to achieve a specific result

- Speak a foreign language to a certain level

- Identify 6 ways to use their time more effectively

- Describe the health and safety policies which apply to their department

They're expressed in this way because then the outcomes are measurable. You can test whether you've been successful.

You shouldn't write objectives in vague terms such as, "The participants will understand..." or , "The group will learn..."

How will you know that they've understood or learned something? Only if they're able to do something with the information. You should make your objectives detailed, precise, specific and measurable.

The sequence leading to the learning objective may be as follows:

1. A training need is identified, e.g. managers in an organisation need to implement a new performance management system.

2. This is turned into a broad training objective:

   "The training will introduce the managers to the company's new performance management system, including the forms to be completed, the timing and format of appraisal meetings and the skills needed to carry out performance reviews."

3. Finally, this leads to specific learning objectives for the course. For example:

4. "Participants will be able describe 4 simple models for giving feedback."

   "Participants will be able to plan an agenda for a performance appraisal meeting using the recommended format."

Some trainers dislike writing out objectives, it can seem a bit of a chore or, at times, the trainer may think, "I know what the course is for, I don't need to write it down."

However, writing out the objectives in this way makes you focus on what the end result of the training will be, what the participants will get out of it. This makes it far easier for you to choose the content which will achieve that result. It also makes it easier to evaluate the training later – if you have clear and precise objectives, you can measure whether people have achieved them.

Outcomes

Learning outcomes are more concerned with the "thinking and feeling" part of the design.

As you can see from the examples above, learning objectives can sound rather dry and sterile. They state what someone should be able to do but they leave out any reference to how they feel about it. I mentioned earlier how important this aspect of learning is – without the right attitude, learning won't take place at all or, if it does, it won't be applied in the way you would like.

How can you plan the way people will feel during and after a course?

In a later chapter I'll take you through 10 ways to get people in a receptive state for learning. This will help you to prepare the right environment and approach to develop a positive attitude in your participants so that they're eager and motivated to learn.

But this is something which you should be planning when you design your training. Think about how the people in front of you are likely to be feeling at the start. How interested are they likely to be, how energised, how enthusiastic?

Now think about how you want them to feel throughout the course and at the end.

What attitude do you want them to have towards the topic you're covering?

For example, you may want them to feel:

- motivated to learn more

- motivated to put into practice what they've learned

- confident about their abilities

- enthusiastic towards the organisation they work for

- supportive towards each other

- energised

- reflective

- concerned, not necessarily worried but aware of the need to take some form of action (e.g. about the environment or about safety)

Thinking about the way you want people to feel may change your approach to choosing the content and the delivery of your training.

For instance, take an induction course. I help to run an induction course for a client. In terms of material, it covers:

- some background to their role in the organisation

- what's expected of them and what they can expect of the firm

- sessions on relevant skills, e.g. personal impact, basic time management, dealing with clients

These areas can be summarised in terms of the learning objectives, covering what they will "know" and be able to do at the end.

However, for some of the people on the course, this will literally be their first two days at work, their first encounter with the firm since they accepted the job.

How are they likely to be feeling when they turn up on their first morning?

Perhaps:

- excited

- anxious

- keen to learn

- worried about what's in store

- hesitant to "expose" themselves early on

- a little doubtful about their abilities

- wondering whether they made a good decision

The firm's attitude towards the course is primarily that the people on it should come to the end of the two days feeling:

- they've had a good time

- they've met some great people

- they've made the right decision in joining the firm

- they're keen to start their careers

This has a huge impact on how the course is delivered. It's high energy, active, fast – moving, varied – and fun! And the impact on how they feel is more important than any of the information which the course covers.

So, if you just read through the learning objectives, you wouldn't get a true feel of what the course is about or what it's intended to achieve.

And this course is in stark contrast to other induction courses I've seen (and been on) which cover "essential" content such as how to complete timesheets and expense claim forms, where to get stationery and detailed outlines of the organisation's structure and hierarchy and result in participants who are:

- bored

- confused

- losing the will to live and

- thinking they've made a terrible mistake.

In summary, you begin to design the content and methodology of your training once you've worked out the detailed learning objectives and also the outcomes in terms of the impact the training will have on the state of mind of the learners.

3 levels of content

Based on the information you've gathered about the needs of the group and the learning objectives and outcomes, you can decide on 3 levels of content:

1. Essential material which the session MUST include to meet its objectives and outcomes.

2. Non – essential but possibly useful information which COULD be included if time permits but not at the expense of the essential material.

3. Material which should NOT be included because it's irrelevant or at the wrong level for the group.

You should be absolutely ruthless when selecting content.

From your knowledge of your subject matter, you'll gather far more potential content than you can include in your course or session. You need to look at each item and test it against the needs of the group and the objectives and outcomes of the course. Then decide which of the 3 categories above it belongs to.

Let me take an example.

I run Transform Your Training courses, amongst other things. The areas I could possibly cover are similar to those outlined in this book, for instance:

- How people learn

- The learning cycle and learning styles

- How to get learners in a receptive state

- How to design your training

- How to ask and answer questions

- How to use activities

- How to use visual aids

- How to handle difficult behaviour

- How to help people remember

However, I don't include all these topics in every course I run. I need to know about the people who are coming, their background and knowledge, why they need the course and what sort of training they do.

Sometimes the group are very new to training and have no background knowledge about how people learn. At other times, the group may be quite experienced and already know about learning theory, they mainly want some new ideas and perhaps some feedback on their delivery skills.

I also need to know how many people there will be and how long the course can last (which usually depends on restrictions of both time and budget for a client).

Once I have that information I can be clearer about the objectives for the training and I can start to select from the range of possible topics and pick out the ones which this particular group will need most.

Vague or fuzzy thinking at this stage will lead to a course which lacks direction or which has too much content and risks confusing people or overloading them with information.

I also think about the outcomes of the course in terms of how I want people to feel. I want them to be energised, enthusiastic about trying new methods, inspired, confident.

How to plan the structure

Once you have the overall content, you need to put it into a structure and work out how you're going to turn the raw material into a training session.

Have a clear, logical development of ideas and break the content down into bite – size chunks. This will stop people being overloaded and it will also give you more opportunities to summarise and repeat your key points.

The subject matter may suggest its own structure, e.g. you may clearly need to explain point A before point B and so on. This is particularly relevant where the content is technical information or where you're training people in a process, e.g. to use software, to operate equipment or to follow a procedure.

I often think it's like remembering the sequence when you're telling a joke. If you miss out a vital piece of information, the punch line will fall flat. You don't want to get to the end and have to say, "Sorry, I forgot to mention, the man in the pub had a parrot."

Work out what people need to know and in what order.

There are other approaches you can take, depending on the subject, such as:

- problem/solution

- present situation/future situation

- question/answer

When you have the overall structure, you can start to design the training course or session itself. This means thinking about how you're going to get the material across to people, including:

- how you'll appeal to different learning styles

- how you'll incorporate the stages of the learning cycle into the training

- how you want people to feel at each stage

- what activities you'll include

- what visual aids you'll use

- what sort of questions you'll ask people

- what balance you'll have between full group discussion, small group work, pair work, individual work, etc.

- how long each part of the course or session will be.

The later part of this chapter will go into more detail about how you should open and close a session and how to break down the material in the main body. Other chapters will cover how to incorporate activities, how to use visual aids, etc.

At this stage, I just want to add what I've found to be a really useful way to look at your overall design and structure. This is to go through your plan for the course and think, "What are the participants doing now?"

The answer could be:

- listening

- discussing in groups or in pairs

- moving around the room

- building a model

- brainstorming

- quietly reflecting

- reading

- being creative

- role playing

There should be variety and there should be participation. Watch out for long sections where the only thing they're doing is listening to you!

How to open a course

Your main job at the start of any course is to get people in a receptive state for learning. I deal with this in detail elsewhere, but to summarise, at the start you need to do four things:

- get their attention

- put them at ease

- clarify what you're covering and what will be happening

- motivate them to get involved

People will have questions in their heads about the training, such as:

- what is this about?

- will this be worthwhile?

- who is this person and what does he/she know about the subject/about us?

- who else is here?

- what's going to happen?

- is this going to be interesting? Is it just going to be a lecture or will we be doing something?

- will I understand this?

- will I have to do anything which makes me look foolish?

You need to answer these questions right at the start and get people feeling comfortable with you and each other and looking forward to the course or session.

So your start should include:

- Something which gets their attention - maybe a good quote, statistic, question, anecdote or appropriate visual aid. This is an opportunity to open with a bang.

  For example, "Do you know how many hours are lost through stress every year? (Pause for thought, then answer.) Well, today you're going to learn some techniques to make sure you don't become part of that statistic."

- Spelling out the benefits of what they're going to learn.

  For example – making their lives or jobs easier, saving them time, saving them hassle or stress, increasing their chances of promotion, giving them more fun or enjoyment.

- "At the end of this course you'll go away with a toolkit of really practical tips which you can use to make your presentations more effective."

- An introduction to you – who you are, your background, what you know about the subject and something which establishes a rapport with your group, i.e. something which shows them that you understand their situation.

- An introduction to each other. Of course, people may already know each other if they all work together and they may bring preconceptions about each other into the training. You need to get them to gel as a group for the purposes of the training so you still need some activity to get them working together.

   Depending on the numbers involved and the nature of the course, you might just ask people to introduce themselves or each other briefly or you might use a group activity as an ice – breaker. I've said more about ice – breakers in the chapter on how to use activities.

- You can decide what you need to know about the group and what they need to know about each other. For instance, you might want to find out their names, jobs or positions, previous experiences, background, how they feel about the course, why they are there, what they want to learn from it. You may also ask for some slightly personal information, such as what their hobbies are or something interesting about them.

- What's expected of them. You want to set the tone of the course, for instance if it's going to be highly interactive, it's particularly important to start with an activity which reflects this so people know they're not going to be sitting around listening to a lecture.

- You may want to establish some ground rules or "group values", e.g. regarding mobile phones, timekeeping, etc. Getting the group to set their own is usually more effective than imposing yours on them.

- Logistics and housekeeping – what is going to happen during the day, the outline and timetable and any administration points that need to be covered, also basic housekeeping such as fire or safety regulations, where the toilets are and any other amenities they may wish to use

This may seem a lot to cover but it's time well invested and it needn't take too long. It's a mistake to take a short cut and just get started with the course content on the assumption that people just want to get on with it. It's essential to get the course off to a good start because, if you haven't got people with you from the beginning, you're not likely to get them back later.

However, do not let the start drag on or become a long list of admin items. Make a point of keeping up the energy, getting people doing something right from the start and getting their attention with a powerful opening.

How to open each session

Of course, you don't need to go through all the items above every time you begin a new session of a course. However, some of them are still vital.

- Even if you've emphasised the benefits people will get from the course as a whole, they may not see the immediate relevance or benefit of each particular session. Spell it out for them and explain why the session you are about to deliver is of value to them. Remind them what they will be able to do at the end of it and why they need to be able to do this.

- Tell people how long the session will be and what you're going to cover. Describe the "map" of the session, i.e. the order of the topics, also what activities they'll be engaged in. For example:

  "First I'll outline the key elements of the new Health and Safety legislation, then you'll split into groups to discuss what impact you think this will have on your work. After that, we'll put together a list of practical steps we can all take to make sure we're working within the new guidelines."

- When introducing material, go from the general to the specific, from the big picture to the detail. The brain likes to make connections between new information and existing knowledge, so help people to make these connections by setting the context for what they're about to learn and showing them where this new information fits into what they already know.

Giving people an overview of what they're going to cover before going into the detail also helps them to identify and remember the key points.

What to do next – the main body

- Follow the "map" you set out at the start. Don't keep it to yourself, remind everyone else where you are going. This helps to keep people on track and also allows anyone who has switched off for a moment (yes, I'm afraid it happens) the chance to find out where you are.

  Use links between the sessions so that you keep reminding people where you've been and where you're going. For example, "Now that we've looked at the main features of the software, let's move on to look at some of the ways you can use it to save time."

- Build in recaps of your main points at the end of each chunk and check that everyone understands before you move on.

- When you're designing your training, build in plenty of variety to keep people interested and to suit different learning styles. For example, consider where to use:
    - visual aids
    - group or pair work
    - movement around the room
    - discussion
    - question and answer sessions
    - brainstorming
    - changes of trainer if possiblegetting the participants to prepare and present information themselves

- Go through your plan of the session and look for ways to make it more interactive and engaging.

- Think about the four stages of the learning cycle and how you will incorporate these into your session. For example, you could use the following steps:

1. An activity relevant to the topic

2. Discussion and reflection on what happened

3. Introduction of some new ideas or approaches related to the activity

4. Discussion of how people would use these ideas to change their approach in future

Alternatively, you could start from a different point:

1. Discuss some ideas about a topic

2. Consider how these could be used to help people in real situations

3. Carry out an activity to let people try out the ideas they've discussed

4. Discuss how the activity went and what people learned from it

Thinking about the stages of the cycle will help you to build variety, activity and discussion into your training and to avoid it becoming a presentation or lecture. It will also help people to learn effectively by taking them through the cycle and it will appeal to all types of learners because it will include something for everyone.

How to close a session

It's amazing how many training sessions just fade away and fail to have any impact at the end. I've heard trainers say things like, "Well, that's about it, unless there are any questions."

This is a wasted opportunity.

People tend to remember what they've heard towards the beginning and the end (a phenomenon called "primacy and recency"), which means that the end of a session is as critical, if not more so, than the start. It's your last chance to drive home the key points and to remind people what they've learned.

- Summarise the key points of the session or, better still, get the participants to do it for you. You can:

  - ask them questions
  - have a short quiz
  - get them to prepare their own summary in pairs or groups
  - ask them to draw a poster on a flipchart representing what they have learned
  - ask each person to give you their own key learning point and what they will do differently as a result

- Ask for questions, but do it in a way which suggests that you really want some, not the usual throwaway, "Any questions?" If you do get questions, don't let the discussion go on too long or people will lose interest and forget the other points you want them to remember. You may need another very short summary after a Q & A session.

Think about ending the session as you started it, with a memorable quote, story or statistic. Alternatively, refer back to what you said at the start to round off the session, e.g., "At the beginning of the session I mentioned that managers spend at least 30% of their time in meetings. You've now learned 10 tips to help you make sure that time is used effectively."

Your 8 step plan for designing a course

1. Identify the specific training need, understand why the training is necessary and what it's meant to achieve. This will give you the general topic to cover.

2. Find out as much as you can about the group you'll be training. Who are they, what do they do, why do they need the training, what do they already know?

3. Determine the learning objectives and outcomes for the training, based on what you want people to think, feel and do at the end.

4. With this information, select the essential content to help this specific group meet these specific objectives. Begin by brainstorming everything you could possibly include, then go through ruthlessly taking out anything which is not essential. If you can't do this, you probably still don't know enough about the group or about the purpose of the training. Go back over points 1 – 3.

5. Work out the overall structure of the course or session, breaking the content into chunks and putting it in a logical progression.

6. Determine how you'll manage the learning for each part of the course or session, i.e. what activities you'll use, what visual aids, what questions, what discussion? Where will you use group work, what will you ask the participants to do?

Make sure you incorporate the four stages of the learning cycle if possible and cater for different learning styles.

7. Design in detail the opening, main body and closing of all sessions. Look at the course as a whole – how does it flow, what are people doing at each stage, how much involves you talking and how much involves the participants being active?

8. Write any supporting materials which you'll need, such as handouts, workbooks or manuals for people to use or take away with them.

How to work with mixed ability groups

Many years ago, when I was a Primary School teacher, it was normal to work with classes or groups of mixed abilities. This presented a challenge to the teacher, how to pitch the lessons and the work so that everyone could benefit, whatever their level.

Many trainers face the same challenge with adults, running technical training sessions for people with different levels of knowledge or skills sessions for people with varying degrees of experience and skill level.

You may also work with groups with a variety of physical abilities or with different levels of English (or whatever language the training will be delivered in).

Some of the approaches I would suggest in these situations will be similar to those I tried to use when I was a teacher.

Here are a few tips:

1. Find out what the range of abilities is as soon as you can. Ideally, find out before the training begins by using pre-course questionnaires or interviews to learn more about your group. Failing that, find out at the start of your session. You can simply ask people or you could use an activity which will give you an idea of the range (you could even have a short test of some sort).

2. One approach is to ask people to line up according to how much they feel they know about the topic, with one end of the line being "nothing" and the other "a lot". Or they could give themselves a mark out of ten. This is, of course, very crude and only gives you an idea of what they think they know, which may be misleading. Still, it's better than nothing.

3. Acknowledge the difference in abilities. Don't ignore it and just plough on regardless. Tell people that you realise there is a range of ability in the room and that you're going to try to give them all something of value, but also ask for their help in making the session useful for everyone.

4. Be clear about what the aims of the training are and what you're going to cover. If it's really not suitable for some people, perhaps you could give them the option of leaving (I know that's not always going to be appropriate).

5. Keep an open mind – don't make assumptions about people's attitudes, abilities or skills, e.g. thinking older

people will be fearful or inept with technology or, alternatively, that they are bound to have come across something before.

6. Determine how much of your training is about presenting new information and how much is about letting people discover for themselves or giving them a chance to process and use information. I spend most of this book encouraging you to minimise the amount of time you spend presenting and increase the activity and this is another reason to do so.

7. If you're spending a long time presenting information, this will cause problems if some of the group already know the information. You have more flexibility if you set up activities where people discover things for themselves or where they can apply what they already know. This will allow people to work at their own level.

8. Mix up the group where you can to allow more experienced or able people to mentor and help the less experienced. Give people an opportunity to share their knowledge, which will also help them to develop it – there is nothing like trying to teach others to make you really think about a topic.

9. Offer a range of activities rather than making everyone do the same thing. This is the basis of mixed ability teaching in schools and is called "differentiation". Prepare tasks at different levels and either allocate groups to tasks or allow them to select their own activity based on which they feel would be of most value to them.

Or you could have a range of tasks which people work through, increasing in the level of challenge, and people can start where they think is appropriate and work their way through, e.g. a range of IT case studies. This also helps to deal with the situation where one group may finish before another because they will have something else to move on to.

I'm told that doctors are sometimes trained or assessed by going round a range of activities in a hall. These may include identifying a body part, making a quick diagnosis, doing a role play where they have to deal with an anxious patient or a written test.

Could you use something like this in your own training?

10. Use various media to allow for different ways of learning and different levels. For example, some information or tasks could be available on the Internet or could involve people carrying out projects online or with audio or video equipment or listening to podcasts or recordings.

Check that you are not using one method of learning which may exclude people with different physical or linguistic abilities. For example, if someone is visually impaired, will they still be able to take part in the learning and have full access to the materials?

11. Check at various points that people are getting value from the training and are happy with the content. Ask for feedback

or have some mechanism whereby people can let you know how they're feeling, e.g. putting smiley or sad faces on a chart, giving marks out of ten. This gives you a chance to adapt what you're doing if it's not working and also shows concern for your learners.

Those are just a few suggestions. I know it all sounds like a lot of work but it may help to make the difference between a training session which is a big success and one which fails to hit the mark and leaves people (including you) feeling frustrated.

Chapter 3: How To Get People In The Mood For Learning

Why is this important?

Imagine you're about to start a training session.

You're standing in front of a small group:

- David
- Jennie
- Ashok
- Sean
- Mark
- Fatima
- Joel
- Helena

Here are some of the things you know about them:

- They're all on a course to teach them about a new software package the company is introducing to help them share information about clients

- They're all at a similar level in the company, Assistant Managers, although they are from different departments

- They'll all be using the new software on a daily basis, replacing a system they've used for several years

Here are some things you don't know about them:

- None of them asked to come on the course. They were all told to come by their line managers. They've not been told anything about the new system or why it's being introduced. They just know the course is something to do with software.

- David has been with the company for many years but hasn't made much progress. He's resentful about this and is looking around for another job. He has no interest in the training as he doesn't expect to be around much longer.

- Ashok hates anything to do with computers. He's anxious about being on the course as he suspects he'll be the slowest one there and he'll be embarrassed.

- Jennie thinks she knows all about computers and software. She's a bit of a "geek" and can't wait to show you how much she knows.

- Sean had a disagreement with his wife this morning. He left home in a bad mood and is still feeling rotten about it.

- Mark is pleased to be on the course because he sees it as a day off work.

- Fatima has a problem with a client which is preying on her mind. She needs to ring him today at some point and she's dreading it.

- Joel has to pick the children up from school today, which means he has to leave by 4.30 at the latest.

- Helena came back from holiday yesterday. This is her first morning back and she has a pile of work to catch up with.

You look out at the group, give a big smile and say, "Good morning everyone..."

How do you think it's likely to go?

I'm not trying to depress you. I'm just making a point about working with adult learners. They're not like young children.

Well, yes they are actually, in many ways. But in some ways they're not.

Adults have a lot of other things going on in their lives, inside and outside work. They don't turn up to a training course with a mind like a blank slate, with no expectations or feelings about it.

And you can't assume that, just because they're there, they've chosen to be there, that they want to learn or even that they know what you're going to be talking about.

- They may be pleased to be there or resentful, partly depending on whether they chose to attend or whether they were sent.

- They may enjoy training or hate it, depending on their previous experiences.

- They may be confident or anxious.

- They may see training as a chance to switch off, to avoid doing any "real work" for a while.

- They may have other commitments which are on their minds and which are more important to them than the training.

- They will always have time pressures (who doesn't?)

They will also have questions in their minds about the training itself, such as:

- What is this about?

- Why do I need to be here?

- What time does this finish?

- Will there be time to check my emails during the day?

- Is this a good use of my time right now? What else could I be doing?

- What does the trainer know about this subject?

- What does the trainer know about me and the work I do?

- Is this going to be interesting or boring?

- What am I going to be asked to do? Am I going to be embarrassed or put on the spot?

- Who else is on the course? Do they know more than I do about this?

- What am I going to get out of this?

- Will there be lunch?

Think of the last time you went on a training course yourself. I bet you had some of these questions in your own mind. I know I do when I'm on a course.

Part of your role is to help people to get into a state where they're receptive to what you want them to learn. Of course, you could take the view that you're doing your job if you just present the material and it's up to them if they don't want to take advantage of it, but I think that's avoiding your real responsibility.

One question I sometimes ask budding trainers is, "If people don't want to learn what you want them to learn, whose fault is it?"

There may be different schools of thought about this, but my own view is that at least part of the fault must be yours. It's not enough to blame the participants for not being in the right frame of mind. An effective trainer will understand that dealing with people's attitudes is one of the first tasks on any training event.

What you need to do is to get people in a receptive state for learning.

What is a "receptive state"?

What is the right state for learning?

To learn effectively, people need to be:

- motivated

- alert

- curious

- relaxed (not too relaxed but not stressed)

- focused

- energized

- interested

They will not learn effectively if they are:

- tired

- bored

- lethargic

- resentful

- resistant

- confused

- stressed

- preoccupied

- distracted

- anxious

- embarrassed

So, you need to do what you can to stop them feeling like this. How do you do that?

Here are my 10 top tips.

1. Know your group

The first thing you can do is to find out as much as you can about the participants before you begin any training.

If you're an internal trainer, this might be easier than if you're from outside an organisation in that you may have easier access to the information. On the other hand, there may be a temptation for internal trainers to assume that they know more than they actually do about the participants.

The least you need to know is:

- Who are they?

- What work do they do?

- Why do they need this training? (Bear in mind that their view may differ from the person who asked you to do the training.)

- What are they expecting?

- What existing knowledge do they have?

- Have they volunteered to come or have they been sent?

- What do *they* want or need to get from the training?

- What are they going to do with what they learn, what difference will it make to them?

Of course, you should be asking these questions anyway in order to determine the right content for the training, but it also helps you to get an idea about their attitude towards it, which is just as important.

If someone has asked you to do the training, you can get some of this information from them. Ideally, also speak to participants themselves. They may see things differently and it will give you a good idea what they are expecting and how they feel about the training.

Alternatively, you could send a short pre – course questionnaire to the participants, asking them about their background and what they'd like to get from the course.

What you're trying to avoid is walking into a room to face a group of people you know nothing about.

Once you have the information, you can be clearer about any possible barriers to learning and what you need to do to get people in the right state.

2. Build positive expectations about the training

Most organisations I've worked in or with have been very poor at this.

The information they send to participants before a course is often very basic, formal and dull. It does nothing to build a positive attitude towards the training, on the contrary, people must read the information and think, "If this material is so boring, what's the training going to be like?"

Even before people arrive for the training, you can be helping them to get into a positive frame of mind.

- Send them information about the course in a "welcome pack". Include an outline of the course and some information about what they will learn. Make sure you set out clearly the benefits they'll get from the training and how it will help them. Your aim is to get them interested and even excited about the prospect.

  Include a short questionnaire to find out more about them and what they want to get from the course. This will show that you're interested in them and in meeting their needs. When they return the questionnaire, send them an email thanking them for it.

  Make the materials attractive and colourful, use pictures and images and write in a friendly, informal style. You could even include other material such as links to short audio or video clips.

There's a list of 10 things you can send people before a course in Appendix 2.

- Try to contact everyone before the course, if only by email, just to introduce yourself and say how much you're looking forward to working with them. This is the start of building a relationship with them.

  If people don't know you, send them a photograph of yourself and some background information. I have a cartoon picture of myself which I send out and many people have commented that they liked the cartoon and appreciated knowing what I looked like so they could recognise me when they turned up to the training. I didn't seem like a stranger to them.

- Give the course an interesting name. General topics such as "Time Management" or "Using Excel" don't grab people's attention. Think of something more intriguing which will get their attention and which is related to the objectives of the training, such as, "How to save an hour a day" or "How to get more done and still go home on time". See this as marketing for the course.

  If it's a technical subject, you could always call it, "All you ever wanted to know about X but were afraid to ask".

If you make an effort before the course, you will already be some way towards getting people in a positive frame of mind before they even arrive.

3. Create an attractive environment

You should make sure that whatever people see when they arrive sets the tone you want it to set.

The room should be inviting and attractive. Some training rooms are like that already but some are glorified broom cupboards which are given over to training because no-one else wants them.

I think my own approach dates back to my time as a Primary teacher. I never wanted children to come into a bare, dull room, even at the start of term when there was no work to put on the walls. I always wanted something that would stimulate and interest them.

Do your best to brighten up the room by letting in as much natural light as possible, putting some flipchart pictures on the walls (and on the door for people to look at as they come in).

You can show:

- some pictures related to the topic

- relevant quotations

- outlines of the day in picture form

- quizzes or puzzles to get people thinking.

This is a great improvement on bare walls. Of course, as soon as possible, get the participants to produce their own visuals to put up as well.

Make sure any tables you use are set out neatly, ideally with colourful materials and any objects you can find that will get people's attention. Look out for items in shops which you can use to brighten up your tables. I've found some excellent mini shopping trolleys which I put on the tables with chocolates and sweets in which are always a talking point.

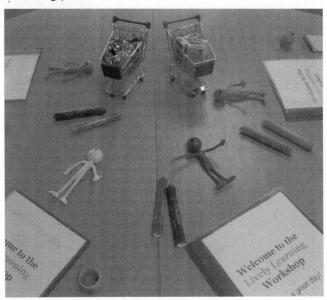

Consider putting out "fiddle toys" for people to use. Common examples are small plastic "slinky" springs, bendy men, PlayDoh or similar putty, coloured pipe cleaners or stress balls.

These brighten up the tables and are also useful for those people who need something to occupy their hands while they're thinking.

Some people develop a theme for a course, for example a travel or sporting theme. They would then decorate the room with appropriate pictures and maybe give participants tickets when they come in. All the materials would follow the same theme. This can liven up some potentially dull subjects and the use of a metaphor (e.g. using the theme of a sporting event to discuss team working) can lead to some interesting learning points.

Warning – one concern when using a theme might be that some people, who have no interest in that theme (e.g. sports), may feel excluded.

I mentioned being neat - make sure you don't leave things around the room, especially at the front, which will make the place look untidy. I have seen some rooms where trainers have left bags, paper, materials, etc. scattered around, leaving the participants to look at a mess all through the training.

The secret is to see the room from the participants' point of view. When you have set things up, go outside and walk towards the room as the participants will. How does it look as they approach? What do they see as they come in? What will their eyes be drawn to first?

What will they see when they sit down and look at the front of the room?

Another thing you might consider is using music to set the tone. I know many people use it. You can use lively music with a thumping beat to wake people up or slow, calming music, depending on what you think is most appropriate.

Either way, it creates a different atmosphere as people walk in. It differentiates the training room from the surrounding environment.

You can also use different music for different parts of the course or different activities. People may come to associate the music with the activity or topic in the way we associate theme music with television programmes. It can also help people to remember.

I must admit I have a few reservations about using music which come from seeing it used unsuccessfully at times. I've seen it lead to discussions about the type of music used (not the constructive kind, more the "What the heck is this?" kind). I've also been on the receiving end of music which was played while I was working and which I found completely intrusive.

Having said that, I know plenty of people who use it so I would suggest having a go and seeing whether it works for you.

Some people go further and put flowers in rooms or use aromatherapy oils to increase the sensory experience. Again, I'd be careful with these because I have an allergy to many flowers and all aromatherapy oils, scented candles, etc. After a few minutes I'd be struggling to breathe. But the idea is sound, i.e. use whatever you can think of to make the room more attractive and create the atmosphere you want.

Whatever you do needs to be appropriate to the group and the nature of the training.

4. Stress the benefits

There is one question which all participants will have on their minds and that is, "Is this going to be worthwhile? Is it a good use of my time?"

You need to address it early on in the training so that people feel motivated to pay attention and to learn.

The key to working with adults is to remember that you can't force them to learn anything.

Adults need to decide that they *want* to learn before they actually will learn. In a sense, you need their permission to try to teach them something. And for that they need a good reason.

Unlike young children, adults tend to need a reason to learn. They don't often learn just for the sheer pleasure of it. Sometimes they do, of course, some people learn an instrument, a language or a skill just because it gives them pleasure. But generally adults want to see some relevance and some purpose to what they are learning.

This is particularly true when the learning relates to work. If they're taking time from their jobs to go to a training course, they need to know that it's going to be worth it and that they're going to learn something useful.

So one of your tasks is to make sure that people understand exactly what they're going to get from the training and what benefit they'll get from paying attention, getting involved and learning.

Part of this is clarifying what you're going to be covering. After all, if people aren't sure what they're going to be learning, they're not likely to be motivated are they?

Right from the start, you need to be explaining very clearly:

- what the training is about

- what it is meant to achieve

- what they will be able to do after the training and

- why that matters to the group.

5. Deal with resistance

People might be resistant to the training for a number of reasons:

- they don't want to be there – they were sent

- they don't understand what it's about

- they don't see why they need it

- for these reasons, they might be thinking of all the other things they could be doing which they see as more important

- there could be other things happening in the organisation which are affecting their attitude, e.g. poor management practices, lack of resources, threat of redundancies

The more you can find out about the people on the course (and the organisation they work for) the better. You may get some clues about how they're feeling and what issues may be affecting them.

But you can't always know everything. Sometimes there'll be issues lurking under the surface which you're not aware of, you may just get a sense that things are not right or there is an "atmosphere".

This is why I feel it's important, if you haven't met the group beforehand, to watch them as they come into the room and see how they relate to each other.

Do people speak to each other, do they smile and laugh together? Do they sit in silence and avoid eye contact? Do they make negative remarks to each other about the course or about work? Are they discussing something that's clearly on their minds which doesn't relate to the course?

These are clues which can help you to judge their mood.

But recognising resistance is one thing, what can you actually do about it?

The first four points above can be dealt with partly by clarifying the content of the training and emphasising the benefits of it, as I've suggested.

You can also show that you understand how people are feeling.

If I have had some idea that people might be a bit resistant, I've sometimes said to a group, "I know you haven't chosen to be here today and some of you may be wondering whether it's the best use of your time. Well, here's what I think you're going to get from being here today and I'll explain why I think it will be worth your time and effort."

I may go further and ask them to elaborate on how they're feeling to bring out any misgivings or preconceptions they have.

That may seem a high – risk approach, but I think it's best to get any potential barriers out in the open. I think it builds your credibility and also your rapport with the group. You're showing that you care about them and that you recognise that what you're doing may not seem the most important thing in their lives.

That isn't to say that you *agree* that the training isn't important. You just acknowledge that they might feel that way, then you take steps to persuade then to change their minds.

If you just carry on regardless, it suggests that you're not interested in them, you just want to get on with what you have to do.

6. Build rapport

Speaking of rapport, I think it's an essential element in creating a responsive group. If you have no rapport, you may as well get your coat and go home. The group won't work with you without it.

What do I mean by rapport?

I mean:

- they like you

- they feel that you're concerned about them

- they feel that you understand them

- they feel that you have some empathy with them

- they feel that you're really trying to deliver something of benefit

If people feel you're trying and you're sincere, they'll forgive you a lot. If little things go wrong, they won't mind.

I once heard an American speaker talking about training, who said, "They don't care how much you know 'till they know how much you care."

Although it sounds a bit trite, I think it's absolutely right. People want to see that you view them as human beings, with their own thoughts and problems, and not just as another group to be trained.

How do you achieve this rapport?

- Be friendly and approachable from the start. Smile at people and talk to them as they come in. Don't hide behind the flipchart at the front or fiddle with your papers, ignoring the group. Speak to them in the breaks and get to know them a little.

- As I've mentioned above, address their concerns. If possible, contact them before the course and find out what they need. Ask them again at the start of the course and show that you're prepared to take their needs into account in delivering the training. This will demonstrate your desire to give them something which is a real benefit to them.

- I've been to concerts where someone in the band has said, "This is the 40th gig on our tour." I don't care about that. I don't care how tired they are or how far they've had to travel. I want to maintain the illusion that they're playing just for me, not just running through a set and not really knowing which town they're in.

You need to do the same – avoid giving people the feeling that this is the umpteenth time you've run this course. As far as possible, tailor the course to them and their needs. People don't want to see you going through the motions, delivering an "off the shelf" course which isn't geared towards their own situations.

- Show that you have something in common with them. People tend to like people who are like them.

You can do this by sharing some experiences you've had which are similar to theirs, especially challenges.

"I remember when I became a manager and I first had to give people feedback, I used to dread it..."

"When I first had to learn this I found it a bit overwhelming but I found the easiest way to approach it was to..."

You can slip these references into your discussions. Don't make them too obvious or it will sound false.

"Hey, look how much we have in common, I'm just like you."

And, whatever you do, don't make things up, just be authentic but draw out any common areas where they exist.

- Use people's names as soon as possible (I feel such a hypocrite saying this, I am terrible at remembering names but, on this occasion, do as I say and not as I do). Refer to people by name from time to time.

"As Jo said earlier." "That's a good point, Dennis."

- Self - deprecating humour works well. Don't take yourself too seriously. Tell some stories about things that have happened to you which illustrate some relevant point and which show that you can laugh at yourself. Don't go too far, you don't want to make yourself look like an idiot! But a few references to times when you made a bit of a hash of things can help to make you look more human and that you don't think you're perfect.

7. Deal with the logistics

Some people will be distracted or preoccupied because they have a lot of other things to deal with, perhaps a pile of work, a call to an angry client or domestic responsibilities.

As I've mentioned, you'll need to spend time stressing the benefits of being on the course so that the group can see how it will be a good use of their time. This will help to some extent.

Another approach is simply to make sure you let people know exactly what is going to happen. They will have questions in their minds such as, "What time does this finish?", "When do we break for lunch and how long for?", "Will there be a break mid – morning?".

This makes it sound as if people can't wait to get out of the training, or they're obsessed with food (both of which may be true). The point is, they may need to take time during the day to make a call, check an email, or carry out some other task which is causing them stress. Someone may need to be sure about the finishing time so they know they'll be able to collect the children from school, for example.

You can help to stop these thoughts from becoming distractions just by giving clear guidelines about the timetable and logistics for the event.

At the same time, you may want to set some ground rules, e.g. that people must switch off mobile phones during sessions (or, if someone is expecting a call they really have to take, they put their phone on silent), or that starting times for sessions must be observed so that, if people do check emails or make calls at lunchtime, they're back on time for the afternoon sessions.

8. Keep up the energy

Stressing, and repeating, the benefits of the learning will help you to counter lethargy. But energy levels will drop at some point during the training, especially if it is a day course or even longer.

The other chapters will give you plenty of ideas to keep people awake and involved, e.g. using visual aids, making learning interactive and using energisers.

The general rule is to keep the training as participative as possible. If people are talking, discussing, asking questions, answering questions, moving around, they can't drop off to sleep.

If people are just sitting listening, doing case studies, reading or using software by themselves for long periods, it's more likely that they'll start to flag a little.

Keep sessions short and punchy, don't let them drag on. How short is short? It depends on what you're doing and how interactive it is. If you're just talking to people, basically presenting information without their being involved (and why are you doing that?), then about 20 minutes will be more than enough.

If a session involves discussion, group work, pair work, etc. then it may take much longer and it won't be a problem.

Even so, people still need regular breaks, for several reasons:

- Some people will need to go the toilet (or the bathroom if they're American – if an English person asks to go to the bathroom, they're probably looking forward to a good soak and playing with the plastic ducks and they may be gone for some time).

- People will need to get up and move around if they're not doing that already – movement keeps blood and oxygen circulating around the body, sitting still doesn't.

- The brain needs time to process information and it does this during breaks - while people are thinking consciously about something else, the subconscious brain is processing what they learned in the session.

Have plenty of water available and encourage people to drink it. One of the main causes of fatigue is dehydration and most people don't drink nearly enough water to keep themselves fully hydrated. Of course, the more water people drink, the more breaks you'll need for obvious reasons.

Build movement into your sessions. Try to find a way to incorporate activity by asking people to move into small groups or work in pairs for a while or, at least, ask people to get up and change seats from time to time.

Some trainers use energisers. These are activities which are not related to the course material, they can just be games or tasks to get people moving and give their minds a chance to switch off from what they are learning (assuming that hasn't happened already).

Be careful with energisers, though – don't use them as a substitute for engaging and interactive training. If the training is lively and active, there shouldn't be much need for energisers.

9. Put people at ease

Some people dread the idea of going on a training course because they worry they'll be asked to do something which either embarrasses them or makes them look stupid.

This may be because they have a low level of confidence generally or because they had a bad experience at some point on a course which has coloured their view of training.

The sorts of things people fear are:

- being asked questions they cannot answer

- being "picked on"

- being made to do something in front of the whole group, e.g. give a presentation

- being asked to do a role play

- having to get involved in some group activity or team game which they find childish or embarrassing

- getting left behind when everyone else is speeding ahead, e.g. on a computer course

How can you avoid this?

Firstly, you make sure people are clear about what they're going to have to do. You explain what's going to happen and what sort of activities will be involved.

For example, "During the session, you'll be spending some time working together in small groups and also occasionally in pairs, discussing ideas."

Then, if you suspect that some activities may cause anxiety, you acknowledge it.

Also, emphasise that it's meant to be a safe and supportive environment where people can ask questions and practice skills without worrying about making mistakes.

If it's not a course where you're expected to give feedback to anyone about the participants, tell them this. Many people assume that the trainer will be discussing them with someone after the course unless you tell them otherwise. This can affect their willingness to get involved, to be open and to take risks.

Explain the reason for any activities. Some people dislike energisers, ice – breakers and (especially) role plays because they see little point in them and they feel silly doing them. They see them as just something trainers do for the sake of it.

However, if you take the trouble to explain the purpose of an activity, most people will accept it and feel less awkward about it. They'll also respect the fact that you treated them like adults rather than expecting them to do something just because you told them to.

Look around the group while you're training to get feedback about how people seem to be reacting. You can get a sense of who may be lacking confidence, who may be anxious or concerned. In some cases, you could have a quiet word in a break if you think someone may be concerned and try to find out what's worrying them.

Above all, set the tone for the training in your own manner. If you appear friendly and approachable, if you seem to know what you're doing, if you show concern for people and treat them sympathetically, you'll go a long way to allaying their fears.

10. Be aware of your own state

So far I've focused on the participants but you must also make sure you're in the right state yourself. Your own attitude will have a huge impact on the learners.

In fact, it could be argued that your state is the one biggest influence on the state of your learners.

If you appear energised and enthusiastic, they'll pick that up. If you seem tired, irritated or uninterested, that's how they'll feel.

- Make sure you're feeling positive about the course and about your ability to deliver it.

- Get plenty of rest beforehand so you have enough energy to keep going all day and inject energy into flagging participants when necessary.

- Be well - prepared. Know your material and have all your visual aids, etc. ready in plenty of time so that you can relax a little and you're not making yourself anxious worrying about it.

- Don't overeat or drink too much the night before the course (which is tempting if you're feeling a bit nervous) or you'll feel sluggish and tired on the day.

- Arrive early for the course to give yourself plenty of time to set up the room and calm yourself down, especially if you have far to travel to the venue.

Chapter 4: How To Use Questions To Promote Learning

Why asking the right questions is critical

Asking questions is the simplest, most basic way to make training interactive and to get away from the presentation or lecture style. Asking questions, at the very least, should lead to a dialogue between the trainer and the participants, which means that they'll always be involved and engaged.

But questions can go much further than that, they can be challenging and stretching, they can form the basis for a form of training which is more like facilitating or coaching.

Facilitating and coaching both mean that:

- your role is to set up activities or discussions which support people in their learning

- you accept that people can learn largely by themselves (rather than needing you to tell them everything)

- you also accept that other people in the room may have knowledge and skills which can help the group, you're not the one with all the knowledge passing it on to a group of people with empty heads waiting to be filled

- you use questions to help people go through their own thought processes in order to come to a realisation or an understanding and to consider how they will use what they are learning

Drawing out what people already know

My own rule of thumb is that I should never tell people anything which I could instead draw out by asking the right question.

A simple example would be, instead of saying, "There are three key elements of a successful training session, these are..."

I should be asking, "What do you think are the key elements of a successful training session?"

This then makes the learners think of ideas for themselves, leads to interaction and discussion and allows the trainer to draw out the key messages instead of spoon feeding learners with information.

You can then follow up with further questions such as:

"What makes these the key elements?"

"How can you build them into your training?"

This is sometimes referred to as "Socratic" questioning, from the practice of Socrates, who used questioning to draw out the knowledge he believed his students already had in their heads.

Introducing new information

If your training involves getting across some sort of technical information which your learners don't know much about at the start, you may think that you can't ask questions.

For example, I used to train people in Tax and, at the start, I couldn't expect that they would know very much about the subject. It would be no use saying, "So what do you think the rate of Corporation Tax might be?"

Obviously, there's little point asking people to try to guess information which they have no way of knowing.

But you can still use questions to:

- introduce the topic

- test people's understanding

- help people think about how they are going to use what they have learned

This is infinitely preferable to just giving a long lecture on the subject and expecting people to absorb large amounts of new information.

To introduce a session on Corporation Tax, for instance, I might ask people what sort of businesses they had come across before, whether they knew anyone with their own business, whether they knew if that was a company or not, how they could tell.

This would get people talking about things they were familiar with and allow them to share their own experiences. It would also help them to see that what we were going to talk about was linked to everyday things they had come across before so it wasn't completely alien to them.

I could use the Socratic method I mentioned above to draw out what people already knew, then introduce the pieces of information I wanted to add as we went along.

How to make sure you get a response

Now you might be thinking, "I understand about asking questions, how hard can that be?" but actually it's harder than you might think. I've seen many people struggle with it.

Sometimes that's because they're so used to just presenting information that they forget to ask any questions. Other times they're asking questions but not getting much response and they don't know what to do about it.

The temptation then is to stop asking questions and go back to just talking yourself to fill the uncomfortable silence. But that's not the answer.

We've all had groups where getting responses was like pulling teeth, but usually there are specific reasons for this. Some may be to do with the group's general attitude to the training, which I cover in the chapter on How To Get People In The Mood For Learning. But it may also be to do with the way the trainer is asking the questions.

What's the right way to ask a question?

This may seem a strange thing to ask, after all, we can all ask questions, but there are ways to ask questions in training sessions which are more likely to get a response.

Allow enough time to answer

A very common mistake is not leaving enough time for people to think of an answer. For example, the trainer might say:

"So what situations have you come across where you could apply this approach?... (short pause)...OK, how about when you're dealing with a difficult customer? Would you use it then?"

What happens is that the trainer asks a question, doesn't get an answer within a couple of seconds, panics and asks another question to see if it has any more success.

The problem is often that he or she just didn't allow enough time for people to think about the first question. This is sometimes the reason why people say they have an unresponsive group. It's not that the group don't want to answer, it's that they're not given time.

How long does it take someone to answer a question?

Of course, it varies, but it nearly always takes a good few seconds. Unless it's something that someone can answer immediately, almost without thinking (and how useful would that be?) there has to be some thought process involved.

This is what that process is like:

"Do I understand this question? Do I have an answer to this question? Am I sure that's a relevant answer? Do I want to share that with everyone else? Do I want to speak?"

That process can take several seconds, especially if it is a question which asks people to share their thoughts or feelings, something personal or maybe something they did wrong in the past.

Stop talking and wait

Once you've asked the question, you need to stop talking and be prepared to stand there for a while, just waiting. Keep eye contact with the group, not in a threatening way, just to show that you're patiently waiting and not in a hurry.

Once they get the idea that you're prepared to wait, they'll take the process seriously and not just give answers off the top of their heads.

While you're waiting and looking around, you can get clues as to whether people are thinking about the question, confused or not bothering to think at all. You can usually tell by their faces.

Who to direct your questions to

When should you direct questions to the group as a whole and when to individuals?

People seem to have different preferences in terms of directing questions to individuals. It is not something I tend to do at all, I prefer to ask the group as a whole.

If a general question doesn't get a response, some people would then move on to individual questions, e.g. "Mary, what do you think about that?"

The purpose of this approach is to try to coax unresponsive people into participating. In my view, whether or not it's effective will depend on why people were unresponsive in the first place.

If it's because they're a bit nervous, then being asked directly might encourage them, but it would have to be done in a very non – threatening manner. The danger is that, if they lack confidence, they won't thank you for making them answer a question in front of everyone else.

If they didn't answer because they couldn't think of an answer, or didn't understand the question, then asking them directly won't help, it will just put them on the spot.

In my view, the only time I would use such a question is when I've been with a group long enough to make a judgement about them and I feel that perhaps someone, who I know is reasonably confident, is just opting out, maybe through tiredness or lack of focus. The direct question would be a way of bringing them back in to the discussion. Even then, I would have to do it in a way which didn't make it obvious I was "picking on them".

However, I know that some trainers use these questions regularly and quite happily, feeling that it keeps participants on their toes if they're never sure whether the trainer might ask them a question.

In the end, it comes down to knowing your group. If you know them well, you're in a better position to make a judgement.

If you do want an individual to answer a question, I'd suggest that you ask the question first, before picking out the individual. That way, everyone hears the question and thinks about it briefly before you ask someone to answer it.

For example, you might ask, "Who can suggest three ways to improve your time management?" Then, if you don't get an answer, you might say, "Peter, do you have any ideas?"

If you start by saying, "Peter, can you tell us three ways to improve your time management?", then the others might switch off, thinking they're off the hook.

Types of questions

There are many different types of question you can ask. Some are more helpful than others in training sessions. It's useful to be aware of them so that you can prepare different questions in advance to suit your purpose and also so that you can check whether you tend to ask the same sort of questions all the time, which can be one reason why a group may be unresponsive.

Closed questions

Closed questions are ones which only require a one word answer, often just "yes" or "no".

e.g. "Do you like ice cream?"

Admittedly, that's not one that often comes up in training sessions so here's another example:

"Do you think closed questions are useful in training sessions?"

That sounds like a question which is inviting some discussion. Unfortunately, it's phrased in a way which makes it closed. Another way of asking the question would be:

"How do you think you might use closed questions in a training session?"

What is the difference? Well, the problem with closed questions is that they do tend to invite one word answers, so that's often what you'll get.

The first question, which starts with, "Do you think...?" will probably get the answer, "Yes" or "No".

In fact, questions which begin with, "Do you...?", "Can you...?", "Will you...", "Would you...?" are bound to be closed questions.

This is useful to know, because if you find yourself starting a question with one of these words, it's a sign that you're heading for a closed question and you may want to rephrase it.

What are some of the other difficulties with closed questions?

Well, if you're asking a lot of closed questions, you'll find that's the problem – you have to ask a lot of them. Because you only tend to get one word answers, there isn't much dialogue going on. You get the one word and then you've got to think of another question. It's hard work!

Also, being on the receiving end of closed questions is frustrating. Let's say that I've just met you and I want to find out about your interests. I try to do this by asking you a series of closed questions.

"Do you like sport?"

"No."

"Do you like watching television?"

"No."

"Do you like going to the theatre?"
"Yes."

"Do you like musicals?"

"No."

The conversation's a bit stilted, isn't it? I'm not learning much, you're not getting very involved in it, it's not very interesting and we're not establishing much rapport. It feels as if I'm filling in a questionnaire.

You may think, "No – one would have a conversation like that" but some trainers do.

They don't mean to, but they ask a series of closed questions to a group and the effect is just the same.

A more natural conversation would include some open questions as well (we'll come on to those in a moment).

So are closed questions any use at all in a training session? (Yes or No?)

It depends.

They can be helpful in some ways.

Sometimes you'll want to open with a closed question to check your starting point. For example:

"Has everyone here had to give feedback on someone else's performance?"

Now that you've checked that you're starting from the right place, you can carry on and open up the discussion.

You might follow that up with a broader question, such as, "What did you find challenging about that?"

Notice that if your next question had been, "Did you find that challenging?", that would have been another closed question and it wouldn't have opened up the discussion in the same way.

You might also use closed questions to check understanding by carrying out a quick test to get rapid answers. For example:

"So now we've looked at the Kolb learning cycle, what was the first stage we discussed?"

This is a closed question, asking for a one word answer rather than a discussion and its only purpose is to do a basic recap of the information.

Open questions

What's the opposite of a closed question?

An open question!

This is one which invites a more expansive answer than just one word. For example:

"What do you think are the qualities of a really effective trainer?"

"How would you prepare for a performance appraisal?"

The advantage of these questions is that they allow for more discussion. They also tend to be more searching questions, making people think harder about the answers. They can also be the basis for small group discussion or pair work.

Open questions can start with words such as "how", "what" or "why".

Of course, it depends on what comes next. The question, "What is the capital of France?" is a closed question. The question, "What are the biggest challenges of running training courses for large groups?" is more open.

A word of warning about "why" questions. You need to be very careful with your tone of voice if you ask, "why". It can easily sound as if you are criticising the person or asking them to justify themselves.

For instance:

"Why would you do that?"

If you use the wrong tone, it sound as if you are asking, "Why (on Earth) would you do that?".

As I've mentioned, the idea is that open questions get people talking while closed questions get little response. In practice, this is a bit of a myth. You can ask some people a completely closed question and they'll talk for hours. With others, you can ask a really open question and get a one word answer.

If you do just get one word answers (and this often happens on the last morning of a long course or in the last session when people are getting tired), don't be tempted to accept them. Use further questions to follow up and draw out more expansive answers. These questions are called...

Probing (or follow up) questions

Probing questions are still open ones, they're just used for a specific purpose – to follow up a previous question.

For example:

"Who's had to give feedback to someone?" (Closed question to check the position.)

Someone puts his hand up (the fool).

"What did you find difficult about that?" (Open question to get him talking.)

"What made that particularly challenging?" (Probing question to get more information.)

As I said above, you can use probing questions to get people to expand on very short answers.

For example:

"What have we discussed so far about adult learners?"

"Receptive states."

"Yes, we discussed receptive states. And what was important about that?"

With a group which isn't being very responsive, the temptation is to stop asking questions and talk more yourself. This lets them off the hook and turns the training into a monologue. Instead, if people just grunt single words at you, use gentle probing to drag something useful out of them.

Hypothetical questions

These are also open questions. They are the "what if..." or "how would you..." questions.

For example:

"What would you do if someone you were giving feedback to started to cry?"

"How would you react if someone came up to your desk and shouted at you in front of all your colleagues?"

One way to use these questions is to help people think about how to apply what they've learned.

For instance, if you've been discussing some ideas on how to manage your time, you might then ask, "So what will you do the next time someone interrupts you when you have got a tight deadline?"

Or you might ask these questions before the training to highlight areas you are going to cover.

For example, if you're training people on some change in employment legislation, you might say, "What would you do if someone was clearly underperforming at work?"

When you had got some replies, you might then say, "Well, yes those approaches would have worked in the past, but from 1 June you would be breaking the law."

This can be a good way to show people how important and relevant the training is because the changes you're talking about apply to real situations.

Multiple choice questions

These are the "Who Want To Be A Millionaire?" questions.

If faced with a hostile group of participants, would you:

    a)   hide behind the flipchart
    b)   offer them sweets and chocolate
    c)   use your highly developed motivational skills to pacify them
    d)   ask if they'd like to try a role play exercise

Like closed questions, these may be useful at times as part of a quick check of people's understanding. But I've seen them used mostly by accident.

Sometimes a trainer will start off a question as a very open one, but then narrow it down to a multiple choice question in an effort to help the group to see what sort of answer is required.

For example:

"How did you feel about that exercise – did you find it easy or difficult?"

What sort of answer are you likely to get? A choice of two words, I would imagine.

Multiple questions

These are not the same as multiple choice questions, which have a choice of answers. These have a choice of questions. They're usually the result of the trainer trying to form the question out loud, maybe starting off with one question, then trying to clarify it or turn it into a better question.

For example:

"How do you feel about the interview process, do you find it difficult, I mean what do you think are the main problems with it?"

Which of those three questions should people answer?

Needless to say, multiple questions should be avoided!

Leading questions

"Lovely day, isn't it?"

"Isn't this a horrible colour?"

"So closed questions probably aren't very useful, are they?"

All those questions are leading questions. What I mean is that they tell you what answer the person wants. They're not really questions at all, they're statements of what the person thinks with an invitation to you to agree with them.

So they're not very useful in training sessions, are they?

Rhetorical questions

"Are we going to put up with this treatment? No, we're not."

"So what are we going to do about this? I'll tell you what we're going to do..."

You'll often find politicians and other public speakers using rhetorical questions. They're used to add emphasis to a speech. The point is that they don't expect or require an answer.

The power of rhetorical questions is to raise the question in the listener's mind, which the speaker then goes on to answer. The device helps the speaker to build a rapport with the listener, a kind of implied dialogue.

We can't help but respond to a question because our brains work that way. We start to think of an answer, even if the speaker doesn't want one. And when the speaker gives the same answer as ourselves, we feel a bond with him or her.

How useful are such questions when you're training?

Well, hopefully by now you'll have got the idea that effective training should not be a presentation or a speech and you should be aiming to get real interaction.

That doesn't mean that there's no place for rhetorical questions, but you need to be careful.

You might well say something like, "So now we've had a look at the new legislation. What difference is that going to make to us in practice? Well..."

You then go on to introduce the next topic.

It can be an effective way to do this because you're probably reflecting the real question which is in the minds of the participants.

The problem arises if you use too many rhetorical questions. What happens the next time you ask a real question? People may not be sure whether it's just another rhetorical one. You may get a few blank looks while people wait for you to continue speaking like you did the last time. It may take them a while to realise and think, "Oh, you really want us to answer that one!"

Using questions as the basis for group work

Of course, not all questions need immediate answers. You can use questions as the basis for group or pair work or for individual reflection.

Take the question, "What are some tips for dealing with angry customers?"

There are various ways you could use this:

- Ask the group to call out answers while you write them on a flipchart

- Give people time to think about the answers individually, preparing their own list

- Ask people to work in pairs for a few minutes to come up with a list

- Put people into small groups to brainstorm ideas

- Get people to write some ideas on cards, then pass them around the group and add to each other's cards as they go around

- Build up the ideas by giving individuals a minute to think of as many ideas as they can, then pair up with someone else to combine their lists, then form small groups and combine them again

There are many other ways to build on this idea.

What might seem a simple question can be the basis for a very interactive brainstorming session. In fact, whole sessions or courses can be designed around the use of a series of questions.

Building your training around coaching questions

What do I mean by "coaching questions"?

Well, coaching is focused specifically on the needs of the person being coached and often involves the coach asking questions such as:

- "What are you trying to achieve? What are your goals?"

- "What difference would it make to you if you could achieve those goals?"

- "What barriers might there be to you achieving them?"

- "What steps do you need to take to start to make those goals a reality?"

- "What internal blocks might there be - e.g. lack of confidence, motivation?"

Coaching also aims to get the person being coached to take responsibility for their own actions and development, not to blame others or give excuses for inaction.

How would using these sorts of questions transform your training?

I've already said that the most effective training is focused on the learner, that it should be interactive and engaging, more facilitation of learning than just presenting information.

Using these questions is a great way to do that. It immediately puts the focus on the learners rather on the trainer or on the content.

It also challenges them to think about what they want to achieve and how they will apply anything they learn.

This can help in transferring any learning back to the workplace, it can stop any training becoming too theoretical or removed from reality and it makes the learners take responsibility for what they do after the training session.

In this way, it can break down potential resistance or any temptation they may have to blame everyone else for any perceived problems they're having.

It makes the participants think more and can be challenging for them, they certainly can't just sit there glazing over.

And it makes YOU, as the person designing the training, think more about how you will focus everything on the learners and how you will structure the event to allow them to ponder on these questions, discuss them and come up with answers.

You can build a whole session around these sort of questions and it will be a very different sort of experience for everyone than if you simply focus on content.

I recently ran a course on Influencing Skills which was built around a series of questions to help participants focus on the specific person they wanted to influence.

In fact, I used to help run a course years ago on dealing with difficult clients on the phone. There were actually no materials at all. We used to go to an office and ask the participants:

- What problems do you have with clients on the phone?

- What are the outcomes you actually want when you speak to clients?

- What are the causes of some of the problems you're having?

- What would it look like if you had the sort of conversations you want with clients?

Then we would run some role play exercises (which they wrote, based on their own experiences) and everyone would chip in with tips about how to handle the situations.

It was a very effective, and popular, course and it involved no preparation on our part other than coming up with good questions to ask at the start.

You could run courses on a lot of topics like that, certainly skills based ones.

(Warning – the reason we were able to do this is because we were all very experienced, both as trainers and in dealing with clients on the phone. So, in fact, we were very well prepared to handle the situations which arose.

For less experienced trainers, this would be a challenge. I am not suggesting that you can just walk into a training room with a list of questions and no thought as to what to do next. You need to be clear what issues you expect to arise, how you will handle the discussions and how you will draw out the key learning points from the group.)

For more technical training, where there has to be a certain amount of information involved, you can use these sorts of questions to make sure you consider how the information will be used when the session is over so that your planning takes into account the needs of the learners.

Then you can use some of them to set up the session - give an outline of the course, then ask people what they want to achieve, what their goals are, etc. to help them to focus on what they want to get from the session and start them thinking. Then keep asking questions whenever they learn something new to make them think how to use what they have just learned.

Once you start to think from the learners' point of view by going through questions like these, your training will never be just a long, one - way presentation of content and you may find that some common problems, such as people losing interest, not responding or not getting involved, will be much less of an issue.

Chapter 5: How To Choose And Use Activities

Why you should use activities

There's an assumption built into many of the chapters in this book that training should be interactive. In other words, the participants should be involved in activities and discussion rather than spending the majority of their time listening to the trainer.

The main reasons for this are:

- the brain needs to interact with new material, to process it and do something with it, in order for it to be understood and retained

- many people learn more effectively by engaging with other people rather than individually, by discussing, debating and sharing ideas

- within any group, there's going to be a pool of existing knowledge and experience (the trainer is not the only person who knows something of value) and interactive training, or facilitating, draws on that knowledge to help everyone learn

- people are more likely to remember ideas they have come up with themselves or discovered through activity than things they have just heard from the trainer

- people are going to be more motivated, energised, interested and involved if they're doing something active rather than sitting still listening for long periods

- group activities involve participants taking some responsibility for their own learning and development rather than relying on the trainer to "spoon feed" them information

- some skills can only be developed through practice with someone else - in a pair or small group

- some people contribute more in small groups than in front of a larger number of people

This means that the presentation or lecture style of training, although still quite common (especially using PowerPoint), is not really appropriate and is less effective than interactive training.

However, using activities is not without its danger. Many trainers fear that they will somehow lose control if they allow people to work in groups. Others struggle to choose appropriate activities or don't put enough thought into how to set them up and debrief them to get the most out of them.

This chapter will give some tips on how to avoid the pitfalls of group activities and it will go through some common examples of types of activity you can use.

6 things you must think about before using an activity

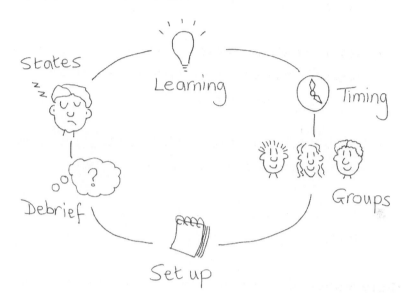

I've seen a lot of trainers come unstuck using activities which they haven't thought through sufficiently. As a result, the following things might happen:

- the activity doesn't raise the learning points which the trainer expected

- the discussion afterwards is rambling and unstructured

- the activity takes far too long and blows the timetable apart

- people get bored and lose interest or get overexcited and lose focus

- the instructions for the activity are too complex and people are left confused

Here are 6 things you need to think about before using any activity.

1. Key Learning Points

What is the point of the activity? What will people learn from it? Are you sure that the activity will lead to the discussion and the learning that you want?

I don't believe that trainers should just set up activities and say, "We'll see what comes out of it, I can't predict, it's up to the group." That seems like an opt-out to me and an excuse for using any old activity on the basis that the trainer doesn't have to say what the outcome will be.

The trainer's skill is in selecting the right activity to lead to relevant learning. And that means being quite specific.

For example, if an activity is meant to illustrate "communication styles", what does this mean? In what context? Does it mean expressing an opinion, giving a presentation, persuading someone to do something, briefing someone? Does it mean communicating one-to-one or in meetings? If you use an activity based on a non-work situation, can you be sure that the principles it brings out also apply at work?

2. Timing

How long will the activity take to set up, run and debrief?

I'll say more on this in a moment but consider how it will work and how long it is likely to take. If you haven't used an activity before, there'll be some guesswork in terms of how much time people will need to complete it. You may need to be flexible - what will you do if people finish sooner than expected or if it takes longer than you thought?

Think through the steps involved. For example, if you split people into 3 groups and ask each group to report back on what happened, how long will you give each group? If they have just 5 minutes each plus 5 minutes for a final review, that's 20 minutes gone for the debrief.

Trainers often underestimate the time it takes to run an activity. As soon as you make training interactive, it takes far longer and you cover less content. That's why you need to strip out unnecessary content and cover a few things in depth.

3. Groups

How will you select the groups - will they be random or do you want them to have a specific combination of people, e.g. those with similar backgrounds or from the same departments or a mixture or "types" in each group?

How big will the groups be? There is often an optimum number for a task, too big and people may be left out, too small and you may not get the learning that you wanted because there aren't enough people to demonstrate some of the points you hoped to bring out.

Linked to this, how many groups do you want? That may be determined by the nature of the activity but also by the amount of space you have and time allowed for debriefing.

Will groups need a leader or an observer and, if so, will you choose that person or will they decide? If the latter, allow time for this.

4. Set-up

How long will it take to set up the activity in terms of explaining it, organising the groups and getting people into place to begin?

I've used activities which were quite complex logistically, involving several groups being in different rooms at specific times and moving around so that timings were critical. These take time to set up and a lot of explanation.

The more complex the task, the more you will need to make sure people understand what is expected of them. Make sure instructions are repeated and written down so that groups have something to refer to.

Also make sure people are clear about the outcome you want, e.g. if they are to report back, do they need a flipchart with notes on or will they report verbally?

5. Debrief

I've touched on this already - how will you debrief the activity?

An activity is only as good as the debrief which follows, which should encourage people to reflect and bring out and reinforce the learning. Don't rush it or be tempted to move on if time is tight.

Look for ways to vary the report back - get people to prepare visuals, sketches, songs or let them choose how they do it instead of the usual "presentation with a flipchart" style.

Your role at the end will be to pull together the learning in some way to make sure all the points have come out and everyone is clear about them. Don't just leave things in the air after a discussion, there needs to be some sort of closing review.

6. The state of your learners

What impact will the activity have on the physical, mental and emotional state of your learners?

Is it a high or low energy activity? Will it get people up and moving, running about and physically active or is it a sedentary one with more discussion and thought?

If people need to be in a certain state to benefit from the activity, how will you get them there? Will they need some sort of warm up to get them ready?

Will they need time to change their state afterwards, maybe to calm down after a high energy exercise?

Does the activity need to come at a certain time in the training, perhaps after people have already had a chance to get to know and trust each other?

Is there any danger of people feeling exposed or embarrassed by the activity (as is the case with some icebreakers and role plays)?

Another element to consider is whether the activity you plan to use assumes a certain level of physical ability, e.g. does it rely on people being able to stand, walk around, run, throw, catch, hear, see? What will you do if there are people in the group who would find it difficult to engage in such activities?

Giving some thought to each of these points will help you to avoid some of the potential pitfalls of group activities and to make sure you use them successfully and with the greatest impact on the learning.

Setting up groups

Some general points about setting up groups:

- Consider whether groups can be allocated randomly or need some planning, e.g. do you want to mix people from different departments or put them in the same group, do you want groups with different personalities or similar ones?

- Try to mix up groups for different activities rather than always using the same ones or they will tend to form cliques and associate more with their own small group than with the whole course.

- Consider using apparently random groupings to separate people who you do not want to work together.

- When briefing participants for a group activity, you need to tell them:
    - what they're going to do
    - the purpose of the exercise
    - what output you want, i.e. do you want them to give a presentation, prepare a flipchart, act out a sketch?
    - how long it will take
    - whether you want them to use any specific process or approach
    - what resources are available
    - whether there are any specific roles for people in the groups, e.g. observer, team leader
    - where they're going
    - what groups they're in
    - when you want them to come back

Explain the activity and the timings *before* telling people the groups and the rooms they need to go to, otherwise they will start moving around and looking for their fellow group members before they know what to do.

(This is one of the ways in which adults are exactly like small children. There are some things we never grow out of.)

- Give instructions several times and have them in writing for people to take with them. There will always be someone who wasn't listening and the first thing anyone says when a group gets together is, "What are we meant to be doing?"

(This is another way in which adults are just like children.)

- As with the start of a session, explain the benefit of the activity, especially where some people may be resistant, e.g. role plays — make sure people know what the point of the exercise is and what they will get out of it.

Pair work

One of the quickest and easiest ways to get participation, especially with a group who do not seem very responsive, is simply to ask them to work in pairs for a couple of minutes. This is very good for generating ideas and for raising the level of energy in the room.

For example, if you want people to think about ways to use activities in training sessions, you could say, "Turn to the person next to you and see if you can come up with 10 ideas in the next 2 minutes."

In my experience, people will always speak to their neighbour if they're asked to, they never sit there and say nothing. Even the most reluctant participant will join in with this.

Also, try setting a challenge, "Give me 10 ideas". This motivates people to try harder. Instead of just putting down four ideas, then thinking, "That'll do", they usually try to reach the target so you get more out of them.

Just be careful about the people you pair up. You may want to split some pairs because you don't think they'll work well together. In that case, find a way to select the pairs, apparently at random, so that you keep certain people away from each other.

Ice - breakers

Why would you use an ice - breaker at the start of a training course? Easy answer - to break the ice, to get people to talk to each other, to help them to settle in. But why do we need to do this? Why does it matter?

Because we want people to feel relaxed and to get to know each other.

Again - why? What does it matter if people feel relaxed? Is "relaxed" the state you want people to be in?

The reason I raise this is because I sometimes see people using an activity at the start of a session or course which isn't necessarily appropriate. They seem to think that you have to use some sort of ice - breaker but I'm not sure they've thought through what they're trying to achieve with it.

I would say one of the main reasons for using an ice – breaker is to get people in a receptive state for learning (not the first time I've mentioned this). By this I mean that they're curious, positive, enthusiastic, energised, confident, open, relaxed.

People don't just turn up in this state, you need to do something to help them get into it.

Used properly, ice – breakers can achieve this. They're also a way for you to find out useful information about the people in the room. You can find out about their background, their experience, their expectations, their attitudes.

An appropriate ice – breaker will allow people to get to know each other in a way which puts them at ease and energises and motivates them.

What is appropriate? It depends on your group and on the nature of the course.

For example - what sort of activities will people be doing during the course? If it is very active and people will be working closely in small groups, you may need an activity at the start which allows them to get to know each other quite well and to start the process of working together so they feel more comfortable later.

If the course will involve people giving each other feedback or sharing some sensitive information about themselves, this is even more important. For example, I run workshops on Assertiveness and Confidence where people will be talking about situations they find very challenging. They need to feel at ease with each other before I can ask them to open up about these issues.

If you're running a technical course, this may not be so vital. However, people will still want to know something about each other, maybe about each other's background and knowledge, so your ice - breaker could help to bring out this information.

Your ice - breaker may reflect the nature of the course in terms of how active, energetic or "off the wall" it is.

For example, if the course is meant to challenge people's assumptions, take them out of their comfort zones or just get them moving around and doing high - energy activities, you may want to use an ice - breaker which reflects this so they get an idea of what is coming.

In short, you need to think through any activity to make sure it's achieving what you want. I've seen activities used at the start of courses which actually made people feel more anxious, embarrassed, self - conscious, resistant and (in some cases) downright hostile towards the trainer because they just weren't appropriate. They asked people to do things they weren't yet prepared to do.

So you need to know your group (as always). You need to know:

- what they expect

- what their attitudes may be to certain activities

- what their likely state will be when they first arrive

- what you may need to do to alter that

- what you need them to be able to do during the course

- how you need them to relate to each other and work with each other

- what information you need to find out about them at the start, e.g. previous knowledge and experience

Then you can start to plan your ice - breaker.

Brainstorming activities

These are activities which are intended to generate lots of ideas about a topic.

The important thing about brainstorming is that the purpose is to generate as many ideas as possible, not to evaluate those ideas. That stage comes later.

For this reason, people should not be allowed to criticise or discard any suggestions, simply to record them, and they should be encouraged to be as creative as possible. No idea should be considered too weird or impractical.

You can brainstorm as a whole group, depending on the numbers, just by asking people to call out ideas while you record them on a flipchart. However, this can get very repetitive and some people will not offer any ideas in a large group.

Here are a few suggestions for other approaches:

- Pair work, as mentioned above. Get people to work together and give them a target for the number of ideas you want in a given time.

- Small groups. As with pairs, put people into groups and ask them to come back with ideas, maybe listed on a flipchart or presented in some other way. Give them all the same topic or give each group a different one.

- Hand out pieces of card or Post-It stickers and ask people to list ideas on them to post up on a flipchart or whiteboard. Get the groups to organise them into themes, remove any which are duplicates and then discuss the remaining ones.

- Get groups to stand in front of a piece of flipchart paper on a stand or on the wall. Ask them to write down one idea on their paper, then get each group to move to the next piece of paper. They can read the other group's idea and add another of their own. This way, people will see each other's ideas as they go along and this will help to spark off new ones of their own.

- Why, why, why, why?

  This approach involves taking a problem, e.g. "Why do our meetings always overrun?" and analysing it by continually asking the question, "Why"?

  For example: Why do our meetings continually overrun?

Because there are always too many items to cover in the allotted time.

Why are there always too many items?

Because we don't have meetings very often so people take the opportunity to raise everything they want to talk about when we do get together.

Why don't we have meetings very often?

And so on. This can help to get to the bottom of a problem and to identify the key factors which contribute to it.

Case Studies

Case studies are a common form of small group work, allowing participants to apply their learning to "real life" situations, to put theory into practice. They may be based on numbers and computations or they may involve writing letters or reports. The main thing is that they reflect the real work people will be doing and they give an opportunity to practice something they have just learned.

Some advantages of case studies are:

- they help people to test and develop their understanding

- they provide a safe environment to practise

- they show the relevance and benefit of what has been learned

- they can help the trainer to test the learning and see where further help is needed

- they can help to transfer the learning from the training room back to the workplace (or wherever people are going to be using it)

However, there can be problems with case studies:

- Like any other approach, they can become repetitive

- They're often the only approach used in certain forms of technical training

- They can be too long and some participants can become bored with them

- They can be too complex, leaving participants confused or frustrated

- They can take a long time to write and may need to be updated regularly

- Participants may complete them at very different rates, leading to time problems or some individuals being left idle while others finish

You can avoid some of these issues with careful planning:

- Don't make case studies unnecessarily long or complicated

- If they do need to be long to be realistic, try to break them up so that people can check their answers at various stages, which will reduce the chances of their getting frustrated if they go wrong

- Make sure a case study only tests the points which are relevant, beware of throwing in other points which may cause problems but which aren't directly relevant to what you've covered in the session

- Allow people to use relevant resources to help them in the case study, e.g. manuals, notes, each other unless there's a very good reason to make them complete it in "exam conditions", i.e. without notes and without speaking to anyone else

- If you think some people may finish early, set some further work for them or have a different kind of activity for them to go and do when they're finished (not just a break or some people may rush the case study because they want to go for a coffee or a cigarette)

Role Plays

The classic role play is where you've been talking about, let's say, giving feedback. Then you practice the skills you've been discussing by getting someone to be the person giving the feedback and someone else to be the person receiving it. You give the two participants a brief explaining their "characters" and then ask them to "act out" the situation.

However, you can also use role plays on a technical course where you ask someone to explain what they've learned to someone else, say a client or customer or someone else in their department who they have to train.

Role plays can be an excellent way to practise skills or to rehearse ways of dealing with specific situations or people. In fact, since the only way to develop a skill is to practise it, role plays are essential on some courses.

They can also be very useful as part of assessment or development centres, i.e. situations where you're assessing how well someone performs at a certain level, perhaps with a view to promoting them.

However, the one thing you must always remember about role plays is that the great majority of people hate them passionately. Nothing strikes fear into the hearts of most people more than hearing the dreaded words, "Now we're going to do a role play". So they need to be handled carefully.

Here are a few tips:

- Explain clearly the benefit of the role play to the participants and acknowledge that they may feel anxious about the prospect.

- Try to avoid using the expression "role play" altogether, use "skills practice" or something similar

- Try to avoid having participants playing someone other than themselves. Use others to play the roles, e.g. other trainers or actors (there are many who offer their services as professional role players) or perhaps other people from the organisation who have not been involved in the course, and let the participants just be themselves

- Make the role plays as realistic as possible and based on actual situations which they'll come across. You can even ask people to write their own briefs for the exercise instead of giving them one yourself.

- Make the exercise as stress – free as possible, e.g. let people practice in pairs or small groups rather than in front of the whole group

- Use a "forum" style of role play. Instead of having one participant working with one role-player, the whole group take part. For example, on a course on "Performance Reviews", the trainer may take the role of the person being reviewed. The group share the task of giving the person some feedback. They can take it in turns or one may start and the others can help out if that person gets stuck. This shares out responsibility and stops one person being the centre of attention.

- Use very clear instructions and written briefs for the exercise

Activities to review learning

One of the key elements in retaining information, in transferring it into the short term memory, is repetition.

No, it doesn't sound very exciting or cutting - edge but there it is. Simple repetition is critical to remembering something.

That means that you need to find ways of repeating the same things when you're training. One of the ways you can do it is to build in various activities which allow people to review what they've learned. The key is to get the learners involved themselves so they're processing the information, which is also important in remembering it, rather than just listening to you.

One of the main ways of doing this is with some sort of quiz, where you ask people questions or they ask each other. But that's not the only approach. Here are 8 ideas for review activities which you can use. Feel free to use them as your own, I've borrowed them from other people myself!

- Snowball fight.

    Get people to write questions about the material on pieces of paper. Then they screw the papers up into balls and throw them at each other (gently) like a snowball fight. When they've finished, each person picks up the ball nearest to him or her and reads out the question, then has to answer it correctly.

- Picture quiz

  A favourite of mine is the picture quiz or Pictionary. This is where you draw a picture representing an idea you've talked about, perhaps even using a visual you've already used. Then people have to say what the idea was and tell you all about it.

- Rather than just drawing your own, you can put people in teams and get them to make up a picture quiz for each other. Or you can get each person in a team to stand up and draw something for his or her team to guess.

- Newspaper article. Put people into small groups and either give each one a topic or give them all the same topic. Ask them to write a short newspaper article about it with a headline. You can give them different papers to copy, e.g. The Sun and The Times, to see what different styles they can come up with.

- Advertisement.

  Get teams to produce a poster or a written advertisement based on your topic. For example, if you've been talking about management, get them to write an advertisement for a manager, setting out the qualities needed.

- Alphabet.

Give groups the letters of the alphabet (or, if you want to make it quicker, give groups a section of the alphabet, e.g. A - F) and ask them to think of a word for each letter of the alphabet which relates to what you've been discussing. The team with X and Z might struggle but people usually think of something!

- Visual aids.

A very simple method, give groups topics and ask them to produce 1 powerful visual aid to summarise the topic, which people could use to remind them of the essential ideas. You could ask them to produce these on pieces of A4 paper, which you could photocopy so everyone could take one back to their workplace with them.

- Sketches or scenes.

Ask small groups to prepare short sketches or scenes to illustrate key points from the training, e.g. good and bad examples of behaviour, client meetings, ways of using machinery or some process. If you have the time and the resources, you could record these on a DVD to keep as reminders (put them on YouTube?).

- A poem or song.

Ask people to make up a poem or a song about the topic. If you have time, you could even ask them to work out an accompaniment using objects to make music (e.g. percussion on the waste paper bin) and add a dance routine.

All these things will add variety and enjoyment to your training and, at the same time, will increase the chances of your learners retaining what they've learned. Using variety will also help you to make sure people with different learning styles can access the material.

Do get the group involved as much as possible because this will make all the difference in the impact of the learning. Also, you'll be amazed at people's creativity. Whenever I ask groups to come up with ideas for visuals, songs, sketches, etc. I'm always surprised at the things they come up with and they're often far more creative and interesting than anything I would have thought up myself.

Reporting back on group activities

When you've asked groups to discuss, or generate, ideas or to go away and practise their skills, you then need to ask them to report back in some way.

Here are 8 suggestions.

a) The most usual method is to ask the groups to write down some bullet points on a flipchart and then get someone from each group to present the information to the others.

A couple of points about this, though. First, if you want people to write points on a flipchart, remember to tell them before they go into their groups, don't just tell them you want them to report back and assume they'll write things down.

Secondly, this method can become rather repetitive if you have several such activities. Also, you have to guard against the same person being the presenter each time. In this case, you may want to insist that groups rotate their presenters.

Some variations on this approach - one problem you get is that, if you ask the first group to report back their thoughts, the other groups may have nothing left by the time it comes to their turn.

One answer is to get each group to give you one point, then move on to another until everyone has contributed.

Another approach is to give the groups different questions to consider around the same topic, so they are covering different aspects.

b) Instead of making a presentation, get the groups to write up their key points clearly and put all the flipcharts up on the wall as a display. Then let everyone walk round the "gallery" and ask questions if they have any, rather than everyone reporting back.

c) Instead of bullet points, get groups to prepare large visual aids which summarise their thoughts and, again, create a gallery where the visual aids are displayed and let people ask and answer questions about them.

d) Ask groups to prepare a summary of their key points in the style of a newspaper or magazine, with a headline and short article. They could type these and print them off or create them on flipcharts. You could allocate styles, e.g. The Financial Times, The Sun, or let them choose their own.

e) Ask groups to prepare a short sketch or play which conveys their key points. These could be good/bad examples of behaviour or common situations they come across at work.Another approach would be to get them to choose a popular TV programme and prepare a sketch in the style of that programme.

f) Groups could report back in the form of an interview, with one person acting as the interviewer and another (or all the others, depending on numbers) acting as the guest being interviewed.

g) The report back could be in the form of a Press conference, where one or more members of the group would give a short statement, followed by questions "from the floor".

h) Ask groups to prepare a short song or poem to perform.

Debriefing activities

On some occasions, you won't be asking groups to come up with ideas so much as to practice something. This may involve doing a case study, working as a team to achieve some task or practicing a skill which they've been learning about.

All activities should be debriefed to help participants complete the learning cycle.

An activity will often represent the "experience" stage of the cycle, the debrief can cover the other 3 stages, drawing out the learning and helping participants to consider the implications of what they've just done and how this may affect future practice.

This may involve giving people feedback on how well they carried out a task and helping then think through what they've learned from it.

Here are some approaches to debriefing and giving feedback.

- Ask people for their own opinion first

- Ask the group, or individual, how they felt the activity went before you give your own opinion.

  People can be very defensive when their performance is being reviewed and they may see feedback as criticism. If you ask them for their own opinions first, this gives them a chance to offer their own view and may put them more at ease.

- It will also give you a chance to see how they feel they've performed and it may give you some clues as to how best to introduce any points you want to make.

- Be specific and give examples

  Describe to someone what you observed and not what you

believe they thought or what you presume their intention was. Tell them the impact this had on you.

This gives you evidence to refer to in order to support your feedback. It also reduces the need for the individual or group to react defensively and gives them something tangible to improve upon.

For example, "I noticed that, when you were engaged in the activity, only three of the group were involved throughout and others tended to stand back and observe. This meant that not all the group had a chance to practice their skills and the activity may have taken longer than it needed to. How do you think this could be avoided in future?"

- Encourage and support first

Give positive feedback before giving constructive criticism. This gives the person or group confidence in their strengths and can make them more prepared to accept feedback on areas that require improvement.

e.g. Positive Feedback: "You've shown great enthusiasm and a willingness to learn."

Constructive Criticism: "There have been times when you've spent too long trying to work things out yourself when it would have been better to ask for help."

However, make sure that your positive comments are

sincere and are not just taken as a sop to "soften up" the person before giving the "real" feedback.

- Don't overwhelm the person with the amount of feedback.

Aim to give people just a few issues to work on. Providing them with a long list of areas for improvement is both confusing and demoralising. Try to balance positive and negative feedback so the person knows what he or she is doing well as well as what needs to be improved.

- Offer some help in improving performance. Don't just offer feedback without adding some comment to help people to improve their performance next time.

For example, don't just say, "Your teamwork was not very effective". Say, "I think you could have worked more effectively as a team if you'd taken some time at the start to find out what relevant skills each team member had and to allocate tasks based on that."

A model for giving feedback

Sometimes it can be useful to have a simple model in mind when preparing and giving feedback. This can help you to pick out the key points to focus on and to deliver the feedback in a structured way.

The EEC Model

E – Example

E – Effect

C – Change or Continue

The EEC model follows the principle that you should pick out clear examples of behaviour when giving feedback and use these to illustrate your points. Then you should offer guidance, either on what the person is doing well, which he or she should continue, or on how to improve their performance in future.

For example:

Example – "When I watched you in the role play giving feedback to the other person, I noticed that you started off straight away by making a negative remark about his performance."

Effect – "The impact of this was that he seemed to be very defensive and quite angry from that point onwards and not very open to the points you were trying to make."

Change – "Next time, you could try asking him first how he felt he was performing and also focusing on positive aspects before moving onto negative ones."

Energisers

I'll say a few words here about energisers, although I have to say I'm not a big supporter of their use. My own view is, if you need to use an energiser to wake people up, why did you let them go to sleep in the first place? If your training is build around interaction and activity, you shouldn't need to use energisers.

Energisers are activities which are used to raise the level of energy at times when participants seem to be flagging:

- Energisers need not be related to the content of the course, in fact they may be more effective if they are not

- They should generally involve physical movement as this is the quickest way to wake people up – people get tired sitting still for any length of time because this restricts the flow of blood and oxygen to the brain

- They may also involve a mental challenge, e.g. a quiz, puzzles, a task or word games

- Energisers, like ice – breakers, need to be suited to the participants and not embarrass them or make them feel silly

- Simple activities such as getting people to change their seats or to stand up and throw a ball to each other can be very effective and quick energisers

Energisers shouldn't be seen as an alternative to making the training itself interactive and interesting. If the course is well designed and structured with appropriate content and regular breaks, there may be no need for artificial energisers.

A good example of an energiser going wrong arose from what I now see as a mistake I made years ago on a course. I asked one of the participants to come up with an energiser to use after lunch on the last day.

After everyone had finished eating, he asked them all to go outside to the car park. During lunch, he'd taken a screwdriver and removed the number plates from all the participants' cars (we were the only ones there at the time so he knew which ones they were). He'd hidden them in the grounds of the hotel.

People went mad. They couldn't believe he'd taken a screwdriver to their nice shiny cars and they weren't pleased about having to search the grounds for their number plates. The activity took ages, especially since he'd forgotten where he'd put most of them (two turned up in a Japanese fish pond).

When they'd finally found their plates, it took a long time to get them focused again, in fact we had to have a break to let them calm down.

Chapter 6: How To Use Visual Aids

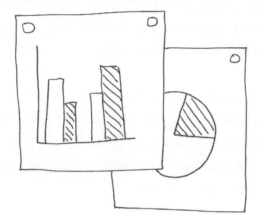

Why use visual aids?

There are numerous reasons why you should consider using visual aids when you're training:

- Visual aids can add impact and emphasis and can aid understanding

- They can reinforce key points and increase people's retention of the material

- A powerful visual image can grab people's attention and help them focus on a key point

- A good visual can illustrate or explain some points more quickly and simply than any words could

- Some people have a strong visual learning style and recall visual images very effectively and everyone uses visual stimuli to learn to some extent

- They can add variety, colour and humour to your training and brighten up a dreary training room if you pin them up around the walls.

In short, information which is supported by clear visual aids is more appealing and will be more easily remembered, but they do need to be *visual*.

For example, photographs, pictures, cartoons, objects, props, people. What about words? Well, you need to be careful with words, words are not really visual, as I'll explain later.

Visual aids are not compulsory, they're there for a reason (which is NOT to take attention away from you).

Whenever you consider using a visual aid, ask yourself, "Will this add impact or aid understanding? How will this support the learning?"

If you're not sure of the answer – don't use it!

When to use visual aids

Once you're clear about the content and structure of your session, you can think about where a visual aid would help people. In choosing the right visual to use, you need to know exactly what you're trying to achieve with it.

Giving statistical information

One of the most common reasons for using a visual aid is to summarise statistical information. A visual aid can show this sort of information much more clearly than trying to describe it in words.

Some examples of this type of visual aid are:

Line graphs

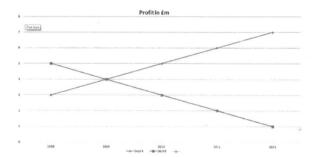

Pie charts

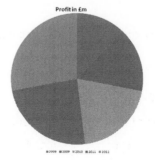

Bar charts

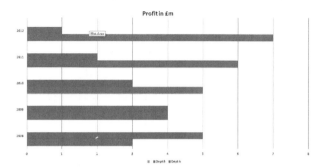

These can be very powerful because they can:

- sum up a lot of information in a clear and concise way

- appeal to people who take in information much more quickly through visual aids than verbal descriptions

- add colour and interest to what might otherwise be a dry recital of facts and figures

- give the information more impact and make it more memorable.

The main thing about these visual aids is that they need to be clear and simple. Make sure that they're not cluttered up with too much information or take too long for people to interpret.

Introducing a topic or moving on

You can use a visual aid to introduce a topic or to mark a transition from one topic to another.

Often these are very basic visuals, what I call representations. What does this mean? Here's an example.

In this case, the visual doesn't really explain much. It shows a computer because the training is about using computers, but other than that it doesn't add a lot. So why use it? Well, it could still be better than nothing.

You might use this visual to:

- add appeal for learners who like to have something to look at rather than just listening

- reinforce the message – just to repeat what you've said in a different way, for instance in case people didn't hear you

- emphasise the fact that you're moving on to a new topic – a new visual aid can mark a transition simply because you put up a new slide or turn over a page on the flip chart (of course, this has less impact if you're using a lot of visual aids because people won't notice so much)

- at the most basic level, just to add a bit of variety and colour, to brighten things up

This simple picture is not the most effective visual aid in the world, is it? It does perform a function, but it's quite a limited one. If you use many of these types of visuals, people will get bored with them quite quickly.

Adding humour

Here's a cartoon I often use to introduce a course on Effective Meetings.

In this case, the visual adds an element of humour. It also says something about how many people feel about the topic.

This might suggest that I have some understanding of the situation the group are in and so it helps to build rapport and establish credibility.

So it's more interesting, it helps to set the tone for the training and it helps to build rapport.

This takes it a stage further than the earlier one.

These sort of "markers", visual aids to introduce a topic, can also be helpful when you're setting out the scope of the session or course. If you show a timetable, for example, with a list of topics, use small visuals to illustrate each topic. Or, as in this case, you can leave out the names of the topics to get people guessing!

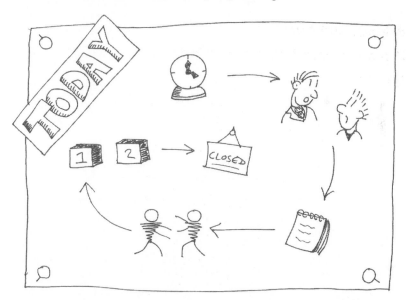

This can help a fairly mundane timetable to stand out, attract attention and be memorable.

In this example, I've used a flipchart but you can do exactly the same thing with PowerPoint if you wish. I'll compare the two later.

Emphasising key points

I mentioned that you would need to decide where to use visual aids to support the learning and an obvious place to do this is where you want to emphasise the key points in any session.

This can be particularly helpful if your key point is based on an analogy.

For example, when talking about the role of the trainer in choosing the right content for a session, I often use the analogy of a sculptor, who has to chip away all the material that he or she doesn't want.

I might then use a picture to illustrate this.

If you want to use visual aids to emphasise the key points, it helps if you don't use too many. If you're constantly showing visual aids, it stands to reason that the impact will be diluted. After all, the idea of emphasis is that you put something extra into it. If this is just visual number 28, it won't have the same effect.

Recapping key points

One reason to show visual aids linked to key points, or even just to topics, is that you can then use them later to help you recap.

You can show a visual aid that you used earlier and ask people to tell you what it represented.

If you used this to introduce the topic, you could go back to it later to use it as a summary of the areas you covered.

You could take the words out, as I've done here, and ask the group if they remember what the three aspects were (although it can be depressing if they don't).

You could then ask people to tell you what the key points were in each area.

You could even not show the visual aid and just ask them "What visual aid did I show at the beginning?" or get them to draw the visual themselves.

Demonstrating "good" or "bad" behaviour

If you're running a skills course or training people to use a process or system of some sort, you can demonstrate the skills yourself, e.g. how to use a piece of equipment or software.

You could also use video clips to show good and bad examples, especially in skills such as giving feedback or time management. You could use professional videos or make your own (I say a bit more on this later).

Of course, you can also use role plays to demonstrate this – these are also visual aids if the other people in the group watch them.

Getting the group to produce visuals

Of course, you don't need to be the only one designing visual aids. One way to increase interaction in your training is to get participants to design their own visuals.

They could do this individually or as a group activity, perhaps to summarise the key points from the session. Ask them to produce their own picture, diagram or poster, for example, explaining something you have been talking about.

Groups can also produce short sketches or role plays to demonstrate skills which they have been discussing, e.g. the right and wrong way to deal with a customer.

This makes everyone draw on their creativity and it will help to make the key points stick more effectively. They will have to review, repeat, process and apply what they have learned in order to produce the visual or the sketch and this means they may well remember the visuals they created themselves longer than the ones you prepared for them.

How to use any visual aid successfully

I'll go into more detail about some specific media in a moment, but here are some general guidelines.

Keep visuals as big, bold and simple as possible.

Don't overload them with information or try to make one visual serve a number of different purposes. People should be able to look at the visual and get the message, not have to work out what it's showing them.

Draw people's attention to visuals when you want them to look, then take their attention back..

Prepare your training session so you can do it without any visual aids if necessary – you don't have to break down just because the equipment does.

Set up your visual aids before your session and sit in different parts of the room to check they're visible from all seats, even the cheap ones.

This is really important – I've seen perfectly good training sessions ruined just because the speaker didn't realise that part of the audience couldn't see properly. People won't always tell you, they'll just stop listening.

Colours

Use dark colours and don't use too many.

Very light colours, e.g. orange, yellow, light green, pink don't show up well on either flipcharts or slides.

If you're using slides, dark colours on a light background are easier to read than light colours on a dark background.

Be careful with colours and what they're associated with. For example, if you write one list of words in red and another in green, people may assume that the red list is "negative" and the green "positive" in some way. If this isn't what you mean, use different colours.

Some people are colour blind and can have problems distinguishing colours, especially red and green.

Words

Words should be used sparingly on visual aids.

- Slides (or flipcharts) which only show words aren't really visual. They don't add emphasis or explain anything more clearly or aid understanding – all the things that visual aids are meant to do.

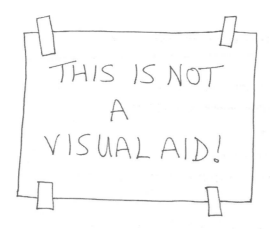

- Real visuals express an idea or concept in a different way. Words are words, whether you say them or project them onto a screen.

- No-one remembers bullet points or words written up on a flipchart or on a PowerPoint slide.

- I've read many guides which state the "6 x 6 rule", i.e. have a maximum of 6 lines of words on a slide and 6 words to a line.
  This suggests that it's OK to use slides with words on, so long as you don't have more than 36 words on one slide. I disagree with this.

  You shouldn't really be using slides with that many words on. In case I haven't made my position on this clear enough, there is more on words - and, in particular, "bullet point syndrome" - when I discuss the use of PowerPoint below (don't say you haven't been warned).

- If you do use words, at least make sure they're legible and big enough to read easily from anywhere in the room.

- On a flipchart, writing needs to be about 4cms high. In PowerPoint, a clear font would be something like Arial 32.

Which visual aid to use?

Choose the form of visual aid to suit the size of audience and the tone of the session.

Flipcharts, for example, are good for smaller groups with an informal tone and where there is more interaction. Interactive whiteboards are also very useful for this and can combine the best elements of flipcharts and PowerPoint.

Projectors (with PowerPoint, slides or video) are good for large audiences and where you want to look more slick and professional.

You may also use TV or computer monitors to show video clips or Internet - based material.

Whatever you're using, don't use technology just because it's there or because someone else is using it.

And don't use a visual aid which makes you feel more nervous because you're not sure how to use it properly.

Also, don't just think of visual aids as flipcharts or PowerPoint – as I've mentioned, you can use:

- whiteboards

- video

- photographs

- cartoons

- props or objects

- glove puppets

- people

- livestock - be imaginative!

One of the ways I used to train people about complex share transactions was to get the group standing up holding different coloured cards which represented different types of shares. I would then talk them through a transaction and they would move around, showing how the shares passed from one company to another. It was very visual and also physical, which is a great combination.

Don't forget that you can create visual images in people's minds through your use of language. Use vivid imagery and colourful descriptions. Tell stories and use real – life examples to help people to picture situations which are relevant to the points you're making.

The right way to use PowerPoint

I must say my heart usually sinks whenever I see someone using PowerPoint.

I'm sure that you, like myself, have sat through some truly awful sessions based on PowerPoint slides.

The problem is, people using PowerPoint nearly always make one (or both) of two mistakes:

1. They use too many slides with too many words on, or

2. They use all the gimmicks that come with the software.

PowerPoint encourages people to use bullet points because it has slide templates which make this very easy.

So, many sessions are simply a series of bullet points slides, one after another after another. Or, worse, they're made up of one huge bullet point slide which slowly builds up as your life drains away.

But slides with bullet points have limited value – they don't add interest, they don't help to explain anything, they just help people to see where you're up to.

Worse than "bullet point syndrome" is the tendency to put whole sentences and paragraphs on slides.

This leaves audiences with a choice – try to read all the information on the slide or listen to the speaker. It's not much of a choice because often the speaker is just reading out the slide anyway.

This also explains why many PowerPoint users spend most of their time with their backs to the audience looking at the screen.

So how do you use PowerPoint successfully?

- Firstly, follow the general principles for visual aids set out above.

- Make sure any slides add impact or illustrate a point – and PowerPoint allows you to do this with all sorts of diagrams and graphs, also photographs and cartoons. You can even build in links to video clips and web pages. But check that everything you use is relevant and don't try to use a clever picture just for the sake of it.

- Keep visuals simple and be aware of the impact of colours and backgrounds.

- Basically, stick to dark colours on light backgrounds and be aware that what looks fine on your computer may not look so good when projected onto a screen.

- Where you do use words, make sure fonts are used consistently, e.g. one for headings and one for text, and don't use too many.

- Also, don't go mad with italics, bold letters, capitals or different sizes. Too many variations will actually make things harder to read.

- Avoid the gimmicks – everyone has seen the slide transitions on PowerPoint and no-one is impressed with them anymore, especially the one where the words fly in from one side and slowly build up into a sentence. (I've even seen someone build up a slide with individual letters flying in - with sound effects!)

- Use Clipart sparingly – most people have seen a lot of Clipart and will react by thinking, "Oh, that one again."

- Think about how you can use PowerPoint to show off its real strengths. As I mentioned earlier, you can show video clips as part of a PowerPoint series, screenshots of computer programmes or include a link to a website. How can you build these into your training?

- Blank the screen if you're not using it for some time so people aren't distracted. Press the B key to black out the screen or the W key to make it white. Then just press the key again to restart.

- Don't look back at the screen while you're talking and, related to this...

- ...NEVER, NEVER, NEVER use the PowerPoint slides as your own notes.

- Find out who's responsible for setting up equipment – it could be you.

- If you're asked for a list of equipment, assume the person who reads it is an idiot – spell everything out, include all the cables you will need as well as the equipment and don't forget the screen. Make sure computers and projectors are compatible.

You MUST run through all PowerPoint slides with a projector before the session.

Slides which look perfect on your computer can change dramatically when shown through a projector. Colours can alter, fonts can mysteriously change size. I've had to go back into PowerPoint programmes at the last minute and make changes because of this. Check all your slides and make sure they're visible from all areas of the room.

Practice with any remote control for projectors. Some have small rubber buttons which can stick when pressed down. Some have a short delay before moving on the slide – you need to know this or you can watch three slides whizz past in one go.

Think about the impact on the energy and attention of the group of turning down lights or letting people watch a long slide sequence. This also applies if you are using videos.

A dark room makes people feel sleepy. If a sequence is quite long, they may expect ice cream at some point.

The right way to use a flipchart

Flipcharts are good for a small group or when you want an informal atmosphere.

They also allow for interaction, e.g. getting ideas from the group and writing them up, or building up a diagram as you speak.
Here are some tips for using a flipchart.

- If you want to build up a diagram or a calculation, for example, on a flipchart, draw it lightly in pencil first so you can see it but the group can't.

- Prepare any flipcharts you're using beforehand to make sure they're clear and neat.

- Take one flipchart sheet and draw lines with a black felt pen 4cm apart. Use this as a guide when you're preparing flipcharts by placing it under another sheet when you write or draw on it.

- I often ask for two flipcharts so that I can use one for my prepared charts and one to use as I'm going along. This also means that I can use the pre – prepared flipchart again.

- Make sure you take your own pens. If you rely on other people, they'll give you special trick pens which are dried up, squeaky or have the wrong colour tops on. Either that or they'll only have orange or yellow, the leftover ones which no – one can read.

- I'd also suggest taking your own paper in case there isn't any supplied.

- Use pictures from various sources to illustrate flipcharts if you can't draw – use simple clipart cartoons or pictures from newspapers.
  Print them off, enlarge them on a photocopier and trace over them onto the flipchart.

- Putting a simple border around your flipchart page can make it much more attractive and focus attention on the contents.

- As well as writing on a flipchart, you can use Spraymount (spray – on adhesive in a can) and then attach cards or pictures to build up a visual.

- Avoid flipchart pads with very shiny paper, felt pens don't write very well on them. Also, check how thin the paper is and whether you can see through one page onto the next. If so, you need to leave a blank page between any pages you've written on.

- If you want to mark a page somewhere on the pad to turn to quickly, either put a Post –It sticker on the page, just sticking out a little, or turn back the corner of the page in front of it so there's a slight gap which you'll be able to see. Then you can turn over the right page without searching for it.

- Beware the flipchart elves!

Tiny flipchart elves visit training rooms every night. As well as stealing all the good pens, they drop the flipcharts down to their lowest settings. This has happened in every room I've ever used, so one of the first things I have to do is raise them up again.

If you don't do this, you will end up having to kneel on the floor to write on the bottom half of the flipchart and most people won't be able to read it anyway.

The right way to use videos or DVDs

There are many professionally made videos and DVDs available on all sorts of subjects, although they tend to be very expensive and also rather generic. Here are some points to be careful about if you use these:

- Check how long the DVD will last. How long do you want people just sitting looking at the screen? Watching a DVD is quite a passive activity and the energy levels in the room can drop while people are sitting there.

- One way to get round this is to split the DVD into sections. Stop it after one section and ask questions about what people have seen so far, such as, "What are the key points you've identified so far?", "Have you spotted any mistakes yet?", "What do you think is going to happen next?"

- Some of these DVDs use well – known actors (or people who have become well – known since making the DVD many years ago). People can be distracted and spend more time trying to spot familiar faces than watching the DVD.

- As I suggested in the previous point, some of these DVDs were made a long time ago. Times may have changed since they were first produced.
  Check the date in any DVDs you use.

- Because most of them were made for a mass market, they may not cover the specific needs or situations of your group. This can lead people to see them as rather irrelevant. You may have to adapt the messages to suit your own purposes or ask people, "So how would you use this information in the real life situations you face every day?"

- You'll need to think about how the DVD fits in with the overall structure and aims of your training. Don't just use it because it's there. I've seen many organisations with libraries of old, dusty videos which they obviously bought some years ago. Trainers can sometimes be tempted to use these just to justify having spent the money.

- Showing a DVD is not an excuse to opt out of the session. You're still in charge, you decide how to use it and why. Remember that it's just an aid, it's not going to do all the training for you. Plan how you'll use it to its best effect, what questions you'll ask about it, what you'll ask people to do before, during and after the DVD to reinforce the learning.

  And, no matter how many times you've seen it yourself, don't sit at the back reading a newspaper while the group are watching it (yes, I've worked with trainers who have done that).

As an alternative to using professionally made videos or DVDs, you could consider making your own simple video using some people from the organisation you're running the course for.

For example, you could interview some people about aspects of their work, good and bad examples they've come across, situations they've been in and how they handled them.

These don't have to be slick, beautifully crafted productions. In fact, it's probably better if they're not. If you just use a fairly basic video recorder to tape an interview with someone, it will have a relevance, an immediacy and an interest factor which no commercially produced video could match.

Using handouts and workbooks

Use simple handouts if these will help people understand the material or more extensive ones where you want them to take away more detailed information, perhaps to expand on areas you didn't go into in much detail during the session.

Consider giving people simple workbooks to follow as you speak. Some people like to have something to write on and to help them concentrate.

- Make workbooks bold and clear, with few words. Use missing words or questions in the materials to encourage people to pay attention – answer the questions as you speak or use them as the basis for group discussion.

- Be careful about giving things out during the session as it will cause disruption and break people's concentration. The only things you should hand out as you go along should be information for case studies or instructions for an exercise which people are going to work on immediately.

- If I give out a workbook at the beginning, I draw people's attention to it and show them what's in it. This answers any questions about whether they need to make notes or not. It also satisfies their curiosity. If I've already shown them what's in it, they don't need to furtively sneak a look while I'm talking.

- If you're giving them detailed information to take away, leave this until the end so people don't read it during the presentation.

- Never give people handouts with your slides on before a session - your slides will lose all impact.

- If your slides are just words, don't use them anyway (see above). If you think people need a handout or worksheet to refer to as they go along, prepare something separately.

Using notes

Notes are your own visual aids. They should be just a reminder of your key topics and point and should be as brief as possible.

They need to be easily accessible and easily visible from a distance. Break up your training into smaller sessions and break up each session into key points.

This will give you the framework and be the basis for your notes. The session headings and the list of key points for each may be the only notes you need.

You can type these out in large print on a piece of paper and have the paper somewhere handy so that you can see the notes easily when glancing down.

Don't put the paper close to a computer or projector as these may blow air out through the side and may send your notes flying around the room.

Use cards if you find this easier than paper (5" x 3" index cards) but remember it may restrict your eye contact and hand movements.

Number the cards and keep them together by punching a hole in each one and tying them with a treasury tag or ring. If you don't do this you *will* drop them and you'll be *so* sorry.

DO NOT use visual aids such as slides as your own notes (yes, I know I mentioned that before – you see how important it is?).

This will encourage you to look at the screen or flip chart, it will also make them less useful for your audience. And if the projector breaks down you will lose your notes.

Write reminders in pencil on a flipchart if you are using one.

You can write notes lightly on the corner of a page so that you can see them when you're turning the page over and remind yourself of the next point. The audience won't be able to see these.

Stop and look at your notes if you get lost or really forget where to go. Taking a few seconds to get back on track gives a better impression than stumbling on when you don't know what to say next.

It's not a sign of weakness that you occasionally have to consult your notes. People will appreciate the fact that you've actually planned the training and that you're concerned about getting it right.

Used well, visual aids can transform a training session, giving it tremendous colour and impact. They can help people to learn and remember and they can add a lot of fun! Be imaginative, use the participants to help to create visuals and draw on their own creativity.

You'll often be surprised at the results.

Chapter 7: How To Help People Remember

Having gone to all the trouble of preparing your wonderful training session, it would be nice if people actually remembered what they were supposed to be learning for more than five minutes after the session ends.

Unfortunately, unless you take steps to help them with this, it's more likely that they'll have forgotten most of what you covered very quickly, if they ever took it in to begin with.

Research (and experience) suggests that, within 24 hours, people may have forgotten up to 70% of the detail of any information they've heard. Within a couple of weeks, they'll have forgotten they ever went on a training course and will pass you in the street without recognising you.

Now that you're thoroughly depressed, I'll give you the good news – there are lots of things you can do to shift the odds in your favour.

Ebbinghaus and his nonsense syllables

Hermann Ebbinghaus, working in the late 19th century, developed a couple of very influential ideas which many trainers quote to this day.

Ebbinghaus set himself the task of remembering lists of nonsense syllables, such as DAX and VOT. He deliberately chose items with no meaning. He memorized them and then tested himself at various intervals to see how well he could recall them.

He found that his recall dropped away sharply after just 20 minutes. After an hour, he had forgotten about half the list and, after 24 hours, he had lost about 2/3.

This led him to set out what became known as the "forgetting curve", showing how new information seemed to be lost from the memory over a relatively short period.

However, he also then set about relearning lists he had previously tried to memorise. He found that, on a second reading of the list, his recall of the items was strengthened and, on a third reading, it was even better.

This led to the idea of "the spacing effect". He suggested that people could be helped to recall information by reviewing it at intervals after their first exposure to it. For instance, they could review it after one hour, after 24 hours and after one week.

This form of review, spaced out over time, was the most effective way to make sure the items remained in the long term memory.

Of course, this work was done a long time ago and it was very early on in the examination of memory. It was also very limited – Ebbinghaus only tested himself, he did not use any other subjects. But Ebbinghaus' work was very influential and seems to be supported by more recent findings.

What follows is a review of some general points about memory and I have listed some useful references at the end of this book if you want to follow them up.

How memory works

It will help you to understand why some of the techniques I'm going to mention are so powerful if you know a bit about how the memory works.

First of all, let me use some everyday examples to illustrate this.

Think of a few times when you've forgotten something. If you're anything like me (and, being human, you are) then you'll have come across these situations:

- Forgetting something because you just had too much to try to remember, e.g. forgetting something from a shopping list which you didn't take the trouble to write down

- Going into a room to do something, getting distracted by something else, then forgetting to do what it was you went in for

- Or simply walking into a room and thinking, "What did I come in here for?" and retracing your steps until you remember

- Forgetting something because you weren't paying attention when someone asked you to do it, what scientists call, "in one ear and out the other" syndrome

- Similarly, forgetting something because you just didn't think it was important enough to remember or because you didn't realise you were supposed to be remembering it

- Having a very clear memory or feeling return because you came across a particular smell or taste

- Remembering very clearly an embarrassing or upsetting experience you had many years ago

- Speaking to someone who obviously knows you but you can't place where you've seen them before and working back in your mind until you remember who they are

These are all clues about how and why people remember or forget certain things.

Deciding what to notice

The first stage in remembering something is noticing it in the first place. If you don't pay attention to something, you're not likely to remember it later.

The brain is bombarded with trillions of pieces of information every single day. It can't cope with all this and it doesn't need to. A lot of information isn't needed, so the brain filters things out. It deals with what it needs to, what's important.

Of course, deciding what's important involves a judgement. There are things which the brain needs to take care of because they relate to your safety or survival. It does some of these things automatically, without your ever being aware of it.

There are other things which may or may not be important enough for the brain to recognise and remember.

Certain things you see every day won't have made any impression on you. Do you remember the colour of the doors of all the houses in your street?

If you walk down the street in the morning, what will you remember about that journey later in the day? Will you remember everything you saw, every person who walked past you, every detail about the buildings, the sounds you could hear, what people around you said?

No, of course you won't. Because you don't need to and you don't want to. In fact, a lot of this information will, in effect, have passed straight through your brain because it wasn't important enough to store.

But, what if you were thinking about buying a new car, say a VW Beetle, and you saw a VW Beetle in the road? What if you were a double glazing salesman and you saw a house with some really old windows? Would you notice those things?

Yes, because your brain would be on the alert for those things, they're things you have flagged as important in some way, as worth paying attention to.

This is why I can remember all sorts of trivia about football matches but forget lots of other things which I'm supposed to be remembering but I'm not really interested in.

So the first thing to be aware of if you want people to remember something is that they have to take notice of it first. They have to see it as important. And, hard as it may be to believe, they may not realise that something you say is particularly important unless you tell them or make it stand out in ways which I'll suggest later.

Where are memories stored?

Memories are stored all over the brain. For example, if you remember a scene from the past, your memory of the sights, the sounds, the feelings and what people said will be stored in different places but will all come together to form the complete memory (or not, if you only remember parts of the experience).

When you have a conversation with someone whom you just can't place, you're having a partial memory of meeting them in the past. You search through your brain trying to find other memories to match up with it so that you can remember who they are.

This point is important in three main ways.

Firstly, different people have different strengths in terms of memory. For instance, some people have a particularly strong visual or auditory memory. Someone with a strong visual memory might recall faces easily or be able to describe what was happening in a scene from the past, but not necessarily what was said. They're also likely to respond better to visual reminders of events or information.

Secondly, this is why associations can trigger off memories. For example, the smell of baking might take you back to a scene from your childhood and the other parts of the memory flood back as well - you can see the scene, hear the sounds.

Thirdly, memories are stronger if all the components of the memory are strong, i.e. if the visual, sensual, auditory, verbal elements are all strong there's more chance of the total memory being easy to recall later.

Emotion also plays a part. If we associate strong emotions with an event, we're more likely to recall it (even if we don't want to). And, when we do remember it, we'll also recall the associated emotion.

I've realised I have a lot of memories of situations where I was embarrassed because I felt I'd said or done the wrong thing and I can vividly recall the place, the scene, the feeling of being there.

How is this important for you as a trainer? If you can involve as many senses and stimuli as possible when someone is learning, the memory will be far stronger. It will also give the person learning more potential triggers to bring back the information when they need it.

Short and long term memory

Short and long term memory are not different parts of the brain. The terms really refer to a process of deepening or strengthening a memory so that there is more chance of recalling it at a later stage. If this process doesn't take place, information may be lost.

When we're taking in information consciously, we have a very limited capacity. We can only handle around 7 pieces of information at once, for example items on a shopping list. If someone starts to give you a list of things to get from the shop, how long does it take before you say, "hang on, I'll write it down"?

You're probably familiar with that feeling of "information overload", when you're sitting in a training session or at a talk and you start to think, "I can't take any more in".

Unless the brain is allowed to process the information in some way, it has to erase some of it to allow more in. The information has to start passing into short term, then long term memory in order to be retained.

For example, suppose someone started reading out a list of numbers from the phone manual. You wouldn't be able to keep them all in your head. You may remember a couple, but you might easily forget everything you heard because there was just too much for you to take in. The information would not even enter your short term memory.

Now think about looking up a phone number you don't know. You remember it long enough to go to the phone and make the call but forget it immediately afterwards. It enters the short term memory but doesn't transfer to the long term memory.

An interesting point here is how you try to remember the number until you make the call. You probably say it over and over in your head. And if someone interrupts you before you can get to the phone, you have to go back to the phone book and start again.

On the other hand, there are probably phone numbers you can still remember from years ago, even though you don't use them any more (perhaps the first phone number you ever had or the number of your first girlfriend or boyfriend).

What causes memories to move from short term to long term? The main elements seem to be:

- Frequency or repetition – this why rote learning can work. Those of us who went through it can still remember our "times tables" from school or lines of poetry we were forced to memorise.

- The combination and intensity of different stimuli and senses, such as sight, sound and smell.

- The opportunity to process or use the information in order to reinforce it, such as applying a formula or trying out a skill.

- Reward and motivation – when we really want to learn and remember something, if we stand to benefit in some way, we have more chance of doing so than if we're not interested.

- Strong emotional associations – think about events you remember from your childhood, why do you remember these and not others? There's a good chance that the ones you remember had a strong emotional connection, such as times when you were very frightened, happy or embarrassed.

- The context or setting in which we take in the information

- Understanding – if we understand what we learn, we can recall it more easily than if we're faced with what seems to be meaningless or isolated information (I remember the difficulty of trying to learn mathematical and scientific formulae at school when I didn't understand what they were for).

- Sleep – believe it or not, sleep helps us to remember. The brain uses sleep time to process and store information. This also applies to breaks between periods of learning when the unconscious brain can work on what has been taken in.

Techniques to use in training

So what does all this mean for you as a trainer?

There are lots of techniques you can use which can help people to take in and remember what you want them to learn. Knowing a little about how the brain works means that you'll understand why these methods are effective and why you need to use them to reinforce the learning.

1. Keep their attention

As mentioned earlier, people need to at least be aware of something before they can remember it. This means that you need to engage and keep people's attention, especially when you're making a key point. Use the techniques discussed here and in other chapters to make sure that any group you work with is focused on what you're helping them to learn.

2. Prepare the ground before you introduce information

You can help people to get the most from any material you cover by preparing them beforehand. For example:

- Review the main topics, give them the "big picture" of what you're going to cover

- Ask them to think of questions they have about the topics which they need answered

- Ask them to say why this information is important and how it will be helpful to them

- Ask them for their own priorities and objectives from each session

You can do some of this by sending out information before the training. It will help to prepare people so that, when they encounter the training material, they are already primed to look for key points and to pay attention to them.

3. Help them to process the material afterwards

The sooner people do something with what they've learned, the more likely it is to stick.

- Ask them questions about it

- Get them to ask you questions or make up questions to ask each other

- Use a case study, a role play or some other method to apply the information in a realistic way

- Get them to discuss what they've learned in pairs or groups

- Get them to summarise the key points of the session using different methods, e.g. by drawing a picture, writing a story, making up a slogan

This works in several ways. It helps people to see the point and the practical application of the information, it allows them to verbalise it and to reproduce it in another form rather than just hearing it and it uses the simple method of repetition.

4. Use repetition and reinforcement

Repetition and frequency are crucial in memory, particularly in passing information from the short term to the long term memory. We all know this, we use it all the time when we repeat things over and over to ourselves to try to remember them.

However, this doesn't mean that you have to resort to the old – fashioned approach of rote learning. This can work, but it's a painful and lengthy process.

Repetition needn't be such a grind. You can repeat points by:

- getting people to rephrase them in their own words or tell you what they think the key points were from a session

- having a discussion about the points

- introducing an activity to illustrate or to apply the points

- letting people work together to explore the points

- asking people to draw posters summarising the points, either in words or in pictures

- making up songs or poems using the information

You need to have regular recaps of the material you've covered.

If you run a one day course, you'll find that, by the afternoon, people will have forgotten some of the main points from the morning. By the end of the day, with no recap, some of what they covered earlier will be a distant memory.

You should break your training up into 1 hour sessions and have a recap right at the end of each session.

If you're running a half day course, let's say, you should have a short recap after each session, then a full recap at the end of the morning.

If you're running a day long course, you should have a recap of the morning's material after lunch, then have a further recap of the material from all the sessions at the end of the day.

These recaps need not take long but they're essential.

Here are a few things you can do (and there are more ideas in the chapter on using activities):

- Simply ask people to tell you what the key points were

- Get each person to tell you their own memorable point or action step from a session

- Give them a short quiz of some kind, perhaps a picture quiz or ask groups to make up questions for each other

- Get people to produce posters or rhymes summarising key points

- Ask people to reflect individually on what they learned from a session and then share something with a partner

Vary the form of the recaps so they don't get boring, but don't underestimate how much will be lost if you don't use them.

Remember to build in plenty of time for them when you plan your training.

You should continue the recaps after the training has finished. Don't just let people leave and then forget most of what you helped them to learn.

You can reinforce the learning by:

- sending out quizzes or short summaries at various points after the training

- giving people access to other material in different forms, e.g. websites, audio tracks, short video clips, social media sites where they can get involved in discussions and ask questions

- helping to create opportunities for people to discuss what they've learned with others and to put it into practice as soon as possible. This may involve working with other people in their organisation to make sure support is available after the training (easier said than done in my experience)

5. Develop understanding

Although simple repetition is important, understanding makes recall much easier. I mentioned that I had to try to learn mathematical or scientific formulae by heart because I didn't understand them. This was much harder work than it would have been if I'd really grasped what they were supposed to do.

Similarly, when I used to run courses to teach people about Tax, I found that people remembered the rules much more easily when they understood why they were introduced, what real situations they applied to and what they were meant to achieve. This gave the information a context and a meaning.

6. Draw out the points from the group

As I've mentioned before, effective training is a form of "facilitation", which means that the trainer's job is to draw out learning or knowledge from the participants rather than just to feed them information. This is done through questioning, discussion and activity.

One advantage of this approach, apart from maintaining interest amongst the participants, is that it takes people through a mental process by which they come to an awareness and understanding of the ideas. People remember things much more easily if they have come up with points themselves rather than being spoon-fed.

For example, you might say to a group, "Here are the four key characteristics of an effective presentation. Number one..."

However, a more effective way to help them learn and remember would be to ask, "What are the four key characteristics of an effective presentation?" and get people to discuss this in groups before summarising their ideas.

Of course, you might not get exactly the four points you thought of yourself, but they would probably not be the only valid ones anyway. And the points which people came up with themselves would be more relevant to them.

This can seem more challenging when you're dealing with factual information rather than "ideas" but even then, with some imagination, you can often find a way of involving the group in the process of discovery rather than giving them everything.

For instance, if you wanted people to know the population of Argentina (I can't think of a reason for this at the moment but I'm sure someone somewhere needs to know this). You could:

- ask them to look up the populations of other countries of similar sizes or other countries in South America

- give them a choice of answers and ask them to discuss the alternatives in groups

- give them some process by which they could work it out, e.g. show them a big map of Argentina with clusters of flags around the main areas, each flag representing 100,000 people

These are ways in which you could lead people towards an answer which would mean more to them (and be more memorable) than just being told.

7. Group related items together

Look at this list:

cod

eagle

elephant

crow

lion

haddock

trout

robin

zebra

swallow

kangaroo

salmon

bear

carp

It looks quite a daunting list to remember, but you've probably already spotted that some items are connected.

Fish	Birds	Mammals
cod	eagle	elephant
haddock	crow	lion
trout	robin	zebra
salmon	swallow	kangaroo
carp	heron	bear

The items make more sense when grouped together and it's easier to remember them. For one thing, it's easy to recall that there are five of each. Even visually, the information seems easier to take in when it's set out in this way. And it would be even easier if the groups were in different colours and there were visual clues next to each word as well.

Wherever possible, help people to see how items are connected rather than presenting them with isolated pieces of information.

8. Create associations

The brain forms connections between pieces of information which are linked in some way and if we remember one of those pieces of information, the others tend to follow.

This is why, if you walk into a room and forget what you went in for, you can remember by retracing your steps back to the place where you first decided to go into that room. The brain associates that place with the thought you had when you were there.

One piece of information acts as a trigger to help you recall another. The more triggers you can give people, the better chance they have of remembering something.

Some people are excellent at remembering names and often use strong visual associations to help them do this. As soon as they hear a person's name, they create a powerful image in their minds which will help them to recall it later. The best example I can think of is a friend of mine who said she remembered a lady called Van Shellenbeck by thinking of a van with a large shell in the back.

People who win memory competitions, the sort of people who can remember 100 phone numbers or random words, often use the idea of a journey to make visual associations. They imagine a route, say moving round the house, going through various rooms and passing specific points. Then they attach each item they want to remember to a point on this journey in some vivid way. Later, to recall the items, they go through the journey in their minds again and, as they see the stages of the route, they recall the items they attached to each one.

Visual associations are an obvious example but you could also use music, rhyme, smells, sound effects or movement.

9. Use mnemonics

A mnemonic is a memory device such as an acronym or an acrostic.

Acronyms are where you use initials to make a word. For example, the acronym AIDA is used in advertising, standing for:

Attention

Interest

Desire

Action

You can ask people to make up their own acronyms as well as giving them your own. This is often more effective.

One problem I find with acronyms is that I often remember the acronym but forget what it stands for (which rather defeats the object). This is sometimes because the acronyms are forced and artificial.

For example, how about this acronym to summarise the key points to remember when you're opening a training session:

Say something interesting to get people's attention
Tell them what you're going to cover
Introduce yourself
Never tell them you're nervous
Know your first sentences by heart

The acronym itself is memorable but the words have been forced in to make it work. In order to work, each initial of the acronym really needs to be the first letter of the key word itself, not the start of a sentence.

Acrostics are similar to acronyms in that they use initial letters, but in this case you use a sentence to remind you of the initials, which then stand for the information you want to remember, such as:

Richard **O**f **Y**ork **G**ained **B**attles **I**n **V**ain

to remind you of the colours of the rainbow.

10. Use rhythm, rhymes and music

Have you ever found yourself singing an advertising jingle and wondered why you can't get it out of your head?

Have you ever wondered why you can remember all the words of songs you heard when you were growing up, which you made no effort at all to learn and never even liked?

That's the power of rhythm, rhyme and music. Put them together and you have a mighty combination. Advertisers know it, songwriters know it, we've all experienced it.

So why don't more people use this in training? Mainly because they feel silly doing it, I suspect, or they worry that their participants will find it childish.

Of course, you need to make a judgement about the people you work with, but I think most groups are quite happy to have a go at this if it's done the right way.

No – one wants to be put on the spot or embarrassed, so it may not always be appropriate to say, "Right, now I want you all to make up a rap to summarise what you've learned and come out and perform it for the rest of the group."

Of course, some people would be happy to do that (some people love karaoke, there's no accounting for taste) but some would be mortified. You need to know your group well enough to know what they'll respond to.

Try asking people to write a short poem or song, to use a well – known tune or to write it in a certain style or simply to come up with some short rhymes to summarise key points.

How about this as a rhyme for safety on aircraft:

"If you hear the engine's missin' please adopt the crash position.

Pretty catchy, don't you think?

11. Give them a rest

Rests and break periods are crucial in learning. When the conscious brain stops focusing on the material, the unconscious brain continues to process it. This is what happens when we sleep and, to a lesser extent, when we simply have a break.

Don't cut back on breaks if you're overrunning. The temptation may be to just press on and cover the material but you'll reach a point of diminishing returns where people start to be overloaded and lose attention.

Even if people say, "Let's miss the break and we can finish a bit early", don't do it. Explain why the breaks are important and stick to them.

You can also offer people something to do during breaks by having some toys or games handy. This helps them to switch off for a few minutes and let their brains do the processing while they're enjoying themselves.

12. Make learning active

From what I've already said about the brain and memory, and from the various ideas I've given about how to aid memory, you'll see that learning and remembering involve people being active not passive. They need to interact with the information they're learning, sitting listening is not enough.

Information needs to be repeated in different forms, it needs to be processed and applied. This may mean people discussing it, asking and answering questions, working in pairs or groups, making up their own visual aids, songs or rhymes, doing case studies or role plays, moving around and carrying out some physical activity.

Your whole approach as a trainer should be to get people as involved and as active as possible. You can find more ideas about how to do this in the chapter on using activities, but it should be built into the design of your training sessions, not just be an afterthought.

13. Make key points stand out in some way

People remember things which are outstanding, perhaps because they're different in some way. For example, look at the following list:

Wren
Heron

Sparrow

DINOSAUR

Lark

Cuckoo

Magpie

Which word are you most likely to remember?

The word Dinosaur stands out because it's larger, in capitals, in bold and it's different from the other words, which are all names of birds.

Of course, you can't make everything stand out. You have to be selective, which means that you need to know what your essential key points are so that you can concentrate on making those memorable.

14. Put things at the start or the end

People remember things near the start or at the end - for example, in a list of items they'll tend to remember the first and last few rather than the ones in the middle. This is called Primacy and Recency (you may remember I mentioned it when talking about opening and closing a session).

This shows the importance of having a clear opening and ending to your sessions which have an impact. These are the times when people will be most likely to take in and remember what you're saying.

Chapter 8: How To Deliver With Impact

I've spent most of this book trying to stress the importance of making learning interactive and getting away from the trainer being a presenter or lecturer and, instead, moving more towards being a facilitator.

However, that doesn't mean that the trainer's own impact is any less important.

How you come across to people will have a huge bearing on how well they respond and how receptive they are to the training.

Your impact depends on 3 things:

- How you look

- How you sound

- What you say

As well as giving some tips on each of these three factors, this chapter will reveal how to handle nerves in order to create the best impact you can. It will also set out some ground rules for working with other trainers to make sure that all those involved deliver their material successfully and don't diminish their impact by getting in each other's way.

Your personal impact

I mentioned above that there are 3 factors which affect your impact – how you look, how you sound and what you say.

Most people spend all their time preparing the third part (what to say) but don't pay enough attention to the first two.

And yet, the first two are more important than the third in terms of persuading people to believe what you say.

Just think of a time when someone said something to you and you could tell by their body language or their tone of voice that they didn't mean it.

For example, you suspect someone you know well is annoyed with you because they're frowning a lot and not talking to you. You ask if you've upset them and they say, " No. I'm fine. " But they don't look fine. Their face tells a different story. And their tone is sharp and abrupt.

There's a mismatch between what they say and the way they say it. And, in those situations, you always, *always*, believe the body language and the tone of voice rather than the words.

How to make a good first impression

This will depend mainly on your visual impact – look confident by establishing eye contact, smiling and looking in control. This is not the time to be searching around for your notes or working out how to plug in the projector.

If you're at the front as people come in, remember that they can see you before you begin, so they'll already be forming an impression. Greet them as they arrive and don't hide away, lurking behind the flipchart or sorting out papers.

Arrive as early as you need to make sure that everything is set up before anyone else arrives. You should have the room ready and be prepared before anyone comes in so that you look relaxed and confident when they see you.

If I'm starting a course at, say, 9.30, I assume that people will arrive from about 9.00 onwards, especially if they're travelling a distance (it's nearly always the case that the people who have to travel furthest arrive first). If I'm not familiar with the room, I would aim to be there by 8.15 to allow time to set everything up.

How you look

Remember that you are your own visual aid and people will be looking at you for quite a long time.

Dress in something which makes you feel comfortable but is at least as smart as your audience (so slippers are out). Think about the impression you want to make.

Avoid wearing anything which will distract people's attention or cause you to keep fidgeting, e.g. dangly jewellery.

Stand up straight with your feet comfortably apart and, initially, with your hands by your sides.

You'll soon move your hands naturally to gesture. If you must hold something, e.g. notes, still use one hand to gesture. Don't try to keep your hands still or you'll look unnatural.

Be aware of how you're standing – if you find you're in a fixed position, move about for a bit. Standing on one spot puts people into a trance, moving keeps their attention. Staying in one fixed position also looks unnatural and makes you seem nervous.

There are four common positions I see people adopt:

- feet apart, hands clasped behind the back

- feet apart, hands clasped together at the front

- legs crossed, feet close together and wobbling

- one hand on your hip

It's not a disaster if you happen to stand in one of these positions, but try to avoid getting stuck there.

When you move, do it for a reason. If you use a flipchart or computer, move towards it when you want to use it, then move away – don't stand next to it the whole time.

Avoid fiddling with something in your hands while you speak. If you find yourself holding a pen, calmly put it down while you're speaking.

Don't put your hands in your pockets. It looks too casual. And, if you're a man, definitely avoid putting your hands in your pockets and then playing with your change while you're talking.

Face the group and keep eye contact. Just keeping eye contact for a second with everyone will have a huge impact. Avoid staring at your own visual aids and, if you use notes, only glance at them.

Not looking at the group is the biggest mistake you can make. It gives the impression that you don't care about connecting with the people you are speaking to or, at least, that you are nervous about speaking.

Also, eye contact will give you valuable feedback about how interested people are and whether they are following what you are saying.

Do not keep looking at individuals or they will start to feel uncomfortable. Up to 2 seconds is probably fine, 3 – 6 seconds and they will wonder why you're staring at them.

How you sound

Speak at a volume slightly higher than is necessary to reach the back row.

This will make sure everyone can hear and it will make you sound confident. It will cover any tremor in your voice and it will help to stop you saying things like "...erm".

Use silence.

Pause to allow points to go home and to add emphasis. Seconds will seem like hours when you're up there, but it won't feel like that to the group. You can easily stop talking for 5 seconds as a short pause.

Make your training interactive to break up the delivery. This will give you a chance for a rest and will allow a natural variety in the pace and tone. This is a good reason to stop for questions as well.

If you tend to speak quickly, as many people do when they're a bit nervous, breaking your speech up with questions or other interaction is a good way to build in pauses.

The problem with speaking quickly is not that people can't understand what you're saying (people can take in words much more quickly than you can say them). The problem is that they need time to absorb the points, to let them sink in. This is where pausing is very helpful.

Speak in a natural, conversational style as if you're just talking to someone you know. Don't adopt a " training voice ".

Keep breathing – deeply from your stomach. Shallow breathing makes you sound breathless and nervous and it inhibits your voice projection. It can also cause you to faint, which may get sympathy the first time but it wears off after a while.

Project a sense of enthusiasm for your subject. Look and sound interested yourself or why should anyone else care?

What you say

Of course, a lot of what you say will be determined by the material you're working with but, in relation to your impact, the main thing is to sound confident and assured and to be clear in what you say.

One of the main points is to speak positively, especially at the start.

Don't say things like, "Hopefully, by the end of this course, you will have learned a few useful ideas."

Instead say something like, "At the end of the day, you'll go away with some very practical tips on how to get more done in less time"

or,

"Today you'll learn exactly how this new computer system works and all the ways in which it can make your life so much easier."

NEVER EVER apologise, tell the group you're nervous or make excuses - for example, "I was only asked to do this yesterday".

It won't get them on your side, it will just make you lose all credibility.

Make your speech as close to normal conversation as possible. Try to give the impression you're speaking to an individual and not addressing a public meeting – use normal expressions and sentences.

For example, don't say, "I will now move on to consider X,Y and Z." No-one talks like that normally. Say, "Now let's have a look at X,Y and Z."

Tell anecdotes from personal experience to make your points more real and interesting and to show their relevance. Stories are also a good way to introduce humour without trying to tell jokes. They can also boost your credibility by showing that you have real experience.

Keep emphasising the benefits of what you're telling people and give them practical applications for the content so they can always see how you're helping them. If they don't see the point of what they're hearing, they'll stop listening.

Try to avoid jargon. Jargon is terminology which only people " in the know " will understand.

All groups have their own jargon. It acts as a sort of shorthand between people who understand it, but it excludes people who don't. The problem is that, if you know a subject very well or you're immersed in a certain type of work, you may well use jargon without realising it.

If you think you might have this problem, ask people to look out for it at the start.

"I'll try not to use any jargon today but, if you do spot me doing it, please shout out and let me know. "

If you want to use abbreviations, e.g. LNA (Learning Needs Analysis, since you ask) then explain the initials first and make sure everyone is clear about what the term means.

How to deal with nerves

What are nerves?

Nerves are part of the body's natural defence mechanism. It is the "fight or flight" response to perceived danger when the body produces adrenalin to help you to either attack or run away.

So it's perfectly normal when you face a stressful situation.

Remember that everyone who speaks in public gets nervous. Even the people who enjoy it can still get " butterflies ".

What happens as you gain more experience is not that you lose the nerves altogether (although they do reduce as you get more practice) but that you realise that the nerves needn't stop you doing a good job.

Instead of fighting the nerves and thinking, "Oh no, I'm nervous again. I can't do it", you just recognise and accept them as the usual sign that you're about to do something mildly stressful – then you get on with it.

Here are some tips to help you to stay calm and to handle the nerves if they do arise.

- Go through your notes and remind yourself of your structure before the start to calm yourself down. Feeling in control of the material is the best way to stay calm.

- Work out exactly what you're going to say when you first stand up.

  This is when you make your main impression but it's also when you feel most nervous. Keep it simple and don't change it at the last minute.

- Never tell the audience that you're nervous.

  They probably won't notice unless you mention it. Nerves are never as obvious to others as you think. Do the simple things right and the nerves will fade quickly.

- Avoid certain things which may emphasise your nerves, such as holding thin sheets of paper which may shake or using a remote control with tiny buttons.

- Arrive early enough to check everything, especially any equipment you're using. Last minute problems will increase your anxiety.

- Think through all the possible problems beforehand (you've probably already done this, that's why you feel nervous).

  What do you think might go wrong? How can you try to prevent this? What will you do if this happens? Thorough preparation, and having a Plan B in case of a mishap, will help to keep you calm.

- Remember that people will want you to be successful.

  Most people will be glad it's not them having to do it and they'll respect you for doing it. They'll give you a chance to do well.

- Go through some relaxation exercises before the session, even if it's just some deep breathing while you're waiting.

  Breathe deeply from your stomach (when you get nervous, you tend to take shallow breaths from the chest and this restricts the flow of air, which can make your voice sound thin and trembling).

- Gentle warming up exercises, as you might do before a sport, can be very helpful to loosen you up (but do these away from the group).

- Remember that it's more important to appear confident than to actually be confident.

  Smile, maintain eye contact and speak with enthusiasm – these are the key ways to appear confident and hide your nerves. Most people who look calm are just bluffing and you can as well.

- Don't expect perfection.

  Some things may go wrong, it's not the end of the world. And it's less likely if you're well prepared. The group doesn't know what you've planned and they won't know if you've missed out something minor or forgotten to use a visual aid, for example.

- Get the group involved wherever possible. Apart from all the other reasons why you should do this, there's the added bonus that it takes the attention off you for a while.

- Talk to yourself in a positive way before you start.

  Tell yourself that you know what you're doing, you're well prepared and you know that you can do this.

Take time to visualise a scene where you're delivering the training and things are going really well. People are listening, laughing, applauding and you're feeling great. Remember a time when you felt confident or when you did something really well and try to recreate that feeling.

How to work successfully with other trainers

You may well find yourself working with other trainers when you're delivering a course. You may do everything as a team or you may deliver alternate sessions.

Working with others can really help to develop your skills and experience (in other words, you can copy their ideas - with their permission, of course).

In fact, there are lots of benefits of working with other trainers, both for yourself and for the learners. You can share tasks, discuss approaches and help each other tackle any problems which arise.

From the learners' point of view, having two trainers adds variety, perhaps offering a change in style, and can allow more personal attention when working in groups.

But it can also go badly wrong!

Have you ever been involved in a course where it's obvious the trainers who are supposed to be working as a team haven't got their act together?

Here are some of the warning signs:

- the trainers contradict each other

- they talk over each other

- or there's an awkward silence where no-one knows who is meant to be speaking

- one trainer does something distracting while the other is leading a session (or reads a newspaper or falls asleep - I've had both happen!)

- there seems to be an element of competition, with one trying to appear more "expert" than the other

- the trainers end up saying more than the learners because each feels he or she has to say something to justify being there

What are the key tips for trainers to make sure they work well together and avoid some of the pitfalls of co-training?

- Trainers should communicate with each other regularly before and during the training, meeting during breaks or at the end of a day to discuss how it has gone and to prepare for the next session.

- They should plan before the event to assign roles, tasks, sessions and responsibilities.

- If one has not run the course before, the other should go through the material with him or her and explain how the course normally runs in practice (which may be quite different from what is set out in the course manual).

- Having said that, the trainer who has run the course before should still remain open to new ideas and different ways of approaching the material.

- Trainers should try not to get too possessive or sensitive about material they may have written themselves (but new trainers should also be sensitive to the fact that things may be done in a certain way for a good reason and not change them just for the sake of novelty).

- Each trainer should keep to the agreed timings and take care not to run over, leaving the other trainer with the problem of making up time or leaving out material.

- Trainers should not contradict each other on important points in front of the learners unless not to do so would cause confusion (e.g. if one makes a serious mistake in what is said). Even then, it should be done tactfully!

- No-one should change the material or the schedule without prior agreement.

- Trainers should agree how each will contribute and behave when the other is leading a session (don't assume that the other person is happy for you to "just chip in" when you have something to say).

- The trainers should be constructive, co-operative and supportive throughout the training (even if they can't stand each other).

So long as these points are followed, co-training can be a very rewarding experience for both the trainers and the learners.

As always, the most important thing is that everything that happens in the training room supports the learning. That's what you're there for, after all.

Chapter 9: How To Set Up The Room

Don't assume that the training room will be set up as you want it. And don't accept a set-up just because it's given to you. The training room is your domain, you decide how it should be arranged.

Having said that, it is very unlikely that the room you're going to use will be set out exactly as you want it, even when you've sent instructions to the venue beforehand. People seem to have different ways of interpreting instructions and what greets you when you walk through the door may bear no resemblance to what you were expecting.

So one of the first things you will usually have to do when you've arrived at a training venue is to start moving furniture around.

That doesn't mean you need to be rude or thoughtless. For example, if you're borrowing a room for the training, make sure you leave it as you found it. If you do move things, put them back when you've finished. If someone has spent time setting things out for you, even if it's not right, be courteous to them and explain why you're changing it.

Why does it matter?

Why is it so important to get the layout right? Because everything in the training room has an impact on the learning. The way people sit, where they sit, who they sit next to, whether they have tables or not, will all affect their attitude to the training, the way they interact and the energy in the room.

Nothing in your training should be left to chance, including the seating arrangements.

Having said that, how do you decide what layout you want?

Here are some questions you need to be able to answer.

- What sort of atmosphere do you want to create - formal, informal, relaxed?

- What will people be doing – listening, watching, reading, writing, discussing, moving around, sleeping, juggling, using IT equipment? Do they need to make notes or draw on flipcharts?

- Do they need to be able to see visual aids?

- Will they be working individually, in pairs, in small groups? Will they be doing role plays? How much do you want them to move around during the session?

- What do you need – do you need a table for notes or a laptop or projector, do you need room to move around, to wander in between the participants?

- Do you want a clear access to the door in case things go badly wrong?

- Will you want to change the layout during the session, to keep up the energy levels and wake people up?

- Will the layout allow full access for people with a range of physical abilities, e.g. is there space for a wheelchair, would the room represent an obstacle course for anyone with a visual impairment?

Bearing those points in mind, here are some of the more common ways of setting up a room, with pros and cons of each.

Boardroom style

The classic boardroom – a long rectangular or oval table with seats all round it. Usually the table is very long, very heavy and you would give yourself a hernia trying to move it.

Pros:

- People have a table to rest on

- I can't think of another one

Cons:

- It's very formal

- You can't walk up and down the centre, you're stuck at one end

- The participants at the other end of the table are usually a long way away and you can't get any nearer to them

- Most of the participants are facing each other rather than facing you

- It doesn't allow for much participation between them or between them and you, it's hard for them to work in groups

- There's no flexibility

- It encourages a presentation style

- People associate it with meetings, which they associate with being bored out of their minds (that's why it is called a "bored room")

Theatre Style

Trainer

Another classic set – up. Rows and rows of chairs with all the participants facing the front. Usually without tables, although sometimes there may be tables or even those chairs with a small table attached to the arm which swings over for the person to rest on.

Pros:

- You can get a lot of people in a room this way (in fact, one thing to check if you're booking a venue is, when they say a room will hold 40 people, for example, do they mean theatre style? If so, it will hold a lot fewer using any of the other arrangements)

- Everyone is facing the front. Having said that, they still may not be able to see you very well if there are a lot of people, unless you are on a stage or a platform

- You can see people quite easily, for instance if someone wants to ask you a question

Cons:

- It's a formal style which many people associate with a lecture or presentation, which they often associate with mind-numbing tedium

- It doesn't lend itself easily to group work because people can't move around

- It's not very flexible, you can't change it if you want people to do anything but look at the front

- People can't see each other, they can only see the backs of other people's heads

- You can't usually move around yourself very easily, you're pretty well stuck at the front. Even if you have room to move around, people won't be able to see you very well

Cabaret style

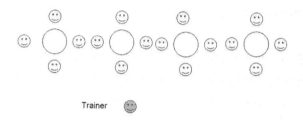

Trainer

Cabaret style involves some arrangement where there are a number of tables around the room and participants sit in small groups around them, e.g. there might be 4 tables with 4 people sitting at each of them.

Pros:

- It's an informal arrangement (assuming that's what you want)

- It automatically puts people into small groups

- It's excellent for encouraging discussion and participation within those groups

- It sets up an anticipation that there'll be group discussion

- You can move around the room and in between the groups if you want

- You can change the focus of the room, there needn't be a clear " front "

- You can change the groups if you want to by asking people to move to another seat, but the arrangement can stay the same

- People have tables to rest on

Cons:

- If it's a cabaret, people may expect you to sing

- Unless you move people around, groups can develop into cliques because people associate with the group they are sitting in rather than with the whole group

- Some people may end up not facing you, wherever you choose to stand, they may be sideways on or even have their backs to you. This may also mean they can't see any visual aids you're using

- Some people may also find it difficult to see the rest of the group, if one table is behind another one, for example. This can make it difficult to get a full group discussion going

- It takes up a lot of room and you can't get so many people into a room as you can with some other arrangements

- It can encourage side conversations, especially if people sit next to their friends (you can avoid this to some extent by asking people to sit in certain places from the start or by moving them around)

U – shape (with tables)

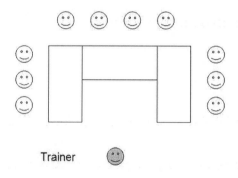

The tables are arranged in a U – shape with the trainer usually standing at one end, the open end. It's a bit like a boardroom but with a gap down the middle and it can vary depending on the length of the tables and the number of people. It can also be a long U or a wide U, depending on how many tables are at the one end.

Pros:

- People have tables to rest on

- If the group isn't too large, this arrangement allows for full group discussion

- Most people can see each other quite easily (depending on numbers)
- It can be quite an informal set – up, again depending on numbers and the size of the tables

- The gap in the centre allows you to move around and in between the participants, which can be useful during discussions or if you need to wake someone up

Cons:

- Some people will be sitting sideways on to you, so it may be hard to get eye contact or for them to see visual aids unless they move their chairs

- round to face you (this is usually possible but some people still won't do it unless you ask them to). If the tables are very long, or if numbers are high, it can share some of the problems of the boardroom arrangement

- Again, depending on numbers, it can be quite a formal arrangement. It can be hard to break people into small groups

U – shape (without tables)

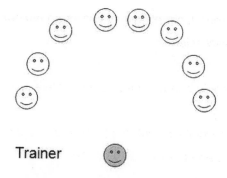

Trainer

In this case, chairs are arranged in a semi - circle but with no tables.

Pros:

- It's very informal and sets the tone for a participative course

- It encourages discussion, participation and openness because people can see each other and there are no tables, which some people think act as barriers

- Everyone can face the front so you can get eye contact and they can see visual aids

- It's flexible, it's easy to move chairs around to make small groups or for pair work or to move them out of the way altogether

- You can move around within the group easily, or even sit as one of the group if you wish

- You can get people to come out to the front, for example to take turns at demonstrating an activity or speaking to the group

- It makes it easy for you to move people around if you wish, as a quick energiser or just to mix people up

Cons:

- Some participants find it unnerving or uncomfortable not having a table, they can feel a little exposed

- More specifically, I've known women on courses say they wish they'd known there wouldn't be any tables, they would have worn something different (i.e. trousers instead of skirts)

- Some people associate this arrangement with some sort of "therapy group" or with what they might call "touchy feely" skills courses. Of course, if they feel like this it suggests they already have some resistance to such courses which will need to be addressed

- There's nowhere for people to rest papers on and it's hard for them to take notes if they want to

- The room tends to get quite messy because people leave things on the floor

- The advantages of the arrangement only apply if the numbers are small

- If the arrangement is in a wide semi – circle, it can be difficult to establish eye contact with the whole group without swinging around from side to side and it can be hard to find somewhere to stand without blocking someone's view of any visual aids you are using

- If you want to put things out for the learners, e.g. workbooks, fiddle toys, sweets, there's nowhere for these to go

Using break – out rooms (or syndicate rooms)

On some courses, you'll want people to work in small groups, perhaps for quite a long time. You may decide to use separate rooms for them to go to, which are called break – out rooms or syndicate rooms (the main room where everyone gets together is called the "plenary room").

Pros:

- It allows small groups to work away from the distraction of other groups

- It adds variety to the set – up of the course

- It adds physical movement, which can energise people

- It allows a change of focus and energy as people move around and sit somewhere new

- It can be an excellent arrangement for role – plays, team games, etc.

Cons:

- You need more rooms, which means more cost if you are hiring rooms

- If the groups need to be supervised, you may need more trainers

- Some people may switch off in small groups if not supervised

- Alternatively, some people may dominate the group

- The rooms are sometimes a distance from the main room, which adds to the time taken for each exercise

- They can also be hard to find in some venues (also, some hotels give you adapted bedrooms rather than training rooms, which aren't always appropriate)

- If the rooms are too far away, there'll be a loss of energy and momentum (and time) as people move around

- It's sometimes good to keep people in the same room for small group work because it builds up a good level of noise and energy, a "hum of activity"

Where will you be?

Don't forget that your own position in the room also has a great impact on the energy and level of interaction.

Consider what you need to be doing at various times

- How much do you need to move around?

- What equipment will you be using?

- Where do any visual aids need to be?

- Do you need a table for your own notes or materials? If so, where will you put it and where will you stand? (Usually try to stand beside, rather than behind a table – unless you really don't like the look of the group)

- Will you stand up or sit down? (Sitting down with a group can help to encourage discussion but, after a while, the energy tends to drop)

- Can you get eye contact with everyone easily?

- Can everyone hear you?

- Will the group be blocking your route to the door if you need to make a quick exit?

There's a lot to think about when setting up a room, so give it some thought before you arrive and don't just accept whatever you find. Don't be afraid to tell people what you need and to change things if they're not right. Try out different arrangements and see what effect it has on your training.

Chapter 10: How To Handle Difficult Behaviour

One of the things which many new trainers seem to fear is that some of their participants will be "difficult".

I prefer to talk about "difficult behaviour" rather than "difficult people" because, in my experience it's very rare that someone deliberately tries to make life awkward for you. What normally happens is that they behave in a way which is not appropriate to what you want to achieve.

For example, someone may not say very much. That doesn't seem very disruptive but it can be a problem where you're trying to get people to contribute, especially if many of the group seem to share this tendency. This is where trying to get participation can be very hard work. You ask a question and get no response.

On the other hand, what about someone who talks all the time, who always has something to say and wants to answer all your questions?

If you're trying to manage a group discussion and involve some of the quieter people, this person can seem a nuisance. However, if you need to raise the energy in the room, or if you need someone you can rely on to make a contribution, you may be thankful for someone like this.

In an earlier chapter, I set out the ways in which you can get participants in a receptive state for learning. Putting those ideas into practice will go a long way towards reducing the chances of encountering difficult behaviour but, if it still arises, this chapter will give you more tips on how to deal with it.

Types of difficult behaviour

Here's a list of the main forms of troublesome behaviour which trainers mention:

- People who talk too much, answering all your questions before anyone else has a chance to say anything or rambling on when they give an answer

- People who don't say anything, never ask a question or answer one

- People who continually ask questions, especially ones which seem to be off the point

- People who challenge what you say ("I don't think that's right")

- People who carry on a conversation with their neighbour while you're talking

- People who play the clown, making jokes and getting others laughing in a way which interrupts your flow

- People who look as if they just don't want to be there, who are disengaged or openly resentful

If you're really unlucky, you'll have a group of 7 people and each one will be one of these characters.

Some trainers have nicknames for different kinds of participants, e.g. "the prisoner" for someone who doesn't want to be there or "the holidaymaker" for someone who sees a course as time off from work and a chance to relax and do nothing.

What is causing the behaviour?

The first point is to be aware that there could be a number of reasons why someone is behaving in a certain way and it can be dangerous to make assumptions.

For instance, what about the person who is not saying anything? This could be because the person:

- doesn't want to be there

- doesn't understand the subject matter

- feels anxious, perhaps because they fear they may be tested on the content or because they don't know anyone else there

- has a learning style which is based on listening to others rather than contributing

- has covered the topic before

- is thinking of something else which is more important than the course

- is bored – this may apply if the person has a preference for an activity - based learning and doesn't like too much discussion

- simply has nothing to say

Notice that none of these reasons has anything to do with wanting to be difficult.

Be aware also that some behaviour may be based in cultural differences and your interpretation of the behaviour you are experiencing may be based on your own cultural references.

For example, in some cultures it is highly unusual for a group of learners to challenge or question anything the trainer says. They may not ask questions, even when they don't understand something, because they feel it would seem impolite.

Similarly, you may find it more difficult in some countries to engage a group in activities or to get them discussing a topic because it is not what they expect or may not be their usual experience of learning situations.

One area I have found to vary very much between cultures is time-keeping. In some countries I've worked in, people's ideas of punctuality have been very different from mine and trying to get everyone back into the training room after a break has been a real issue.

This is another example where the behaviour itself may be challenging, even though the people involved aren't deliberately trying to be difficult.

So how can you know what to do if you don't know what the cause of the behaviour is?

There are two answers:

1. you try different things to see what works and/or

2. you ask them.

I'll say more about these approaches below.

Beware the "tipping point"

Certain behaviour, such as people having private conversations or continually interrupting you, will disturb the rest of the group.

They'll have noticed the behaviour and, at this stage, they'll probably want you to do something about it. And, up to a point, you'll have their support in dealing with it.

However, you need to be careful how you handle the situation.

You're walking a tightrope between keeping order and maintaining rapport with the group.

If you deal with it in a heavy – handed way, if you are sarcastic or if you embarrass the person involved, the group may close ranks behind the individual and turn against you. You'll be seen as having attacked one of their own and you'll lose their support and any rapport you've built up.

This is what I call the "tipping point", when the group suddenly moves from backing you to supporting the other person.

It will be quite obvious if this happens. There'll be something like a communal intake of breath and the atmosphere will turn very icy. You'll suddenly find that people are avoiding eye contact or not saying very much.

Some approaches I will mention are more high risk than others in terms of how likely they are to take you over this "tipping point". In the end, you have to use your own judgement based on how well you know the group.

6 approaches to any situation

There are some specific things you can do to deal with each of the difficult behaviours I listed above but first I want to cover some general approaches which are relevant to all situations.

1. Manage the activities, or the set – up, to work around the problem without drawing attention to it.

This is low risk because no – one realises you're trying to deal with a particular person's behaviour.

For example, if you find that some people are not contributing to group discussions or answering questions, ask the group to work in pairs for a few minutes to think about a point. This will always get people talking, whatever the reason for their previous silence.

It also gives you a chance to watch them with their partner. If the person seems to be talking quite happily in a pair, then they probably just felt self – conscious about speaking in front of the whole group. If they still look concerned, it may be that they don't understand the topic and you can deal with this later.

If someone has been hogging the discussion, it stops them (at least temporarily).

If two people have been holding their own conversation, this will interrupt them (unless you happen to have the two of them working in a pair, but you can avoid this).

Another approach might be to change the seating arrangements.

As a quick energiser, I sometimes ask people to stand up and then sit down at least two seats away from the people they were sitting next to before. This takes a minute and gets people moving around. It also rather cleverly splits up any participants who've been talking to each other.

2. Use your body language.

This might be apparent to the participants or not, depending on how you do it.

For example, if you want someone to contribute more, you could let your eye contact dwell on them a bit longer when you ask a question.

Alternatively, if someone is answering every question, you can avoid eye contact with them for a while, look towards other half of the group when you're waiting for an answer. This can subtly encourage others to contribute.

You can use movement as well. If two people are talking to each other, you can move in their direction while you're talking. Depending on the layout of the room, you might even stand quite close to them (without saying anything to them or looking at them). They'll often be aware of your presence and stop talking. Again, no- one will necessarily notice that you've done anything.

You may decide to raise the stakes a little if this doesn't work and make it obvious that you're waiting for them to stop talking. You might look directly at them or even stop talking yourself while standing near them so that they get the message.

This, of course, is higher risk because it's obvious that you're doing something. It's unlikely to turn the group against you but it does mean you have to do something if the pair don't stop talking because everyone knows that you've seen it and your authority is on the line.

3. Speak to the person in a break.

Whatever the behaviour which is causing you problems, one approach you can always try is to talk to them about it during a break.

Of course, you need to think what to say to them. I'm not suggesting you go up to them and say, "Now look..."

However, this is an opportunity to find out what's behind the behaviour.

For example, with a quiet person, you might start by just asking them how they're finding the course so far. They may just say, "Fine" or they may volunteer the fact that they've covered this material before or that they're struggling with it. This gives you an opportunity to discuss it with them.

For instance, if they say they've covered it before, you might say, "Well, I hope it's been a useful recap for you. We're moving on now to look at X. Is that something you've come across before?"

If they say, "Yes", get them to tell you a bit more about when they covered it and how. If possible, tell them how this will be different or ask them to help you out by contributing to the discussion to share their knowledge with the others.

If someone has continually been talking to their neighbour, you might just point out that you've noticed this and ask whether they have a problem they need to discuss with you, if there is something they don't understand.

If they say, "No", you may need to be quite direct and just say that their talking is disturbing some of the others (and you) and could they leave any private conversations until the breaks.

The advantage of speaking to someone in a break is that you can do it away from the others, so once again it's not apparent that you're taking action, which reduces the risk of it backfiring.

4. Speak to the person in front of the group.

In this case, you're making it obvious that you want some behaviour to change.

You might say to someone who hasn't spoken, "David, you haven't said much yet, what do you think?"

Or, to someone who answers all the questions, "Andrea, you've answered a lot of questions so far, let's give someone else a chance."

Or, if people are talking to each other, you might just say, "Would you mind having that conversation later?"

How well this works depends largely on how you say it. It can be the easiest way to tackle the situation and cause no problem whatsoever – if you say it in a way which is still friendly and not antagonistic and if you've built up a good rapport with the group.

You may even use humour and (high risk) a touch of sarcasm if you know the group well and you're sure you can get away with it.

However, this is treading a fine line. A colleague of mine told me of a situation where he tried this. He thought he'd built a really good relationship with the group, they'd shared a laugh and there was a relaxed atmosphere – until he made a sarcastic remark to one of the group.

He said, "I thought it would be OK, we'd been laughing and everyone was friendly. But, as soon as I said it, I wished I hadn't. It didn't come out as I intended, it came across as a bit harsh and the whole atmosphere instantly turned frosty. All the rapport had gone and I never got it back."

5. Question your own approach. Are you doing something which is contributing to the behaviour?

For example, if people are looking disinterested or starting to talk to each other, is it because the content isn't at the right level or there isn't enough variety in the delivery? Maybe a discussion session has just gone on too long or maybe (perish the thought) you've been talking too much.

Maybe people need a break or a change. If the group isn't responding to questions, perhaps the questions aren't clear.

6. Send them home!

And, as a final (very high risk) strategy, you can always ask someone to leave the course!

I've done this once in all my years of training, when someone was being very disruptive and I'd already spoken to him about it. I finally said (in a break), "Look, you clearly don't want to be here and you're disrupting what I'm trying to do. Do you think it would be best for everyone if you just went back to the office?"

He didn't. Why? Because he would have had to explain to his Boss why he'd been sent back early. However, it worked in as much as he sat there fairly quietly for the rest of the course.

Specific behaviours

These general approaches will cover pretty well any situation you come across but here are some ways in which you can tackle specific behaviours which are causing you problems.

The silent one

- Make eye contact regularly

- Look approachable, smile and be friendly

- Introduce some pair work, then ask that person to report back what they discussed (this puts them on the spot less than asking them a direct question such as, "Julie, what do you think about this?")

- When organising group work, ask different people to take the lead in reporting back

- Remember that there's no rule that says everyone needs to speak equally during a course. Consider whether someone being quiet is actually a problem at all

The miserable one

- If you sense that the whole group are unhappy about something (such as being on the course), then you might consider bringing this out into the open to deal with it (as I suggest in the chapter on getting participants in the mood for learning).

  However, if it's just one participant who looks as if he or she doesn't want to be there, don't allow them to vent their feelings in front of everyone else. People like this can be toxic and spread their misery around.

- Avoid the temptation to ignore the person or to pick them out by saying, "Cheer up, it can't be that bad." You'll only draw attention to them. Treat them like everyone else. If they start to show other behaviour, e.g. talking to their neighbour, then use one of the other techniques described in this chapter.

- If the person starts to voice negative opinions during discussions, change the type of questions you ask to more factual ones or bring in another activity for a while to avoid giving them a platform to express their discontent.

- Speak to the person in a break and find out how they feel about the course. They'll probably tell you. It may be that they don't see the point, they think they have heard it all before, they were told to come by someone they don't like or even that they've just given their notice in and they're leaving the next week (I've had that happen more than once). Or it could be that they have some problems which are nothing to do with the course.

Once you know what's behind the behaviour, you can deal with it, e.g. by stressing to them what they'll gain from the course and, if appropriate, by showing some understanding of their position.

The know – all

- Use eye contact and body language to (subtly) cut the person out of your eye line for a while when you ask a question.

- Acknowledge the person's status as an "expert" by thanking them for their contribution and saying, "you clearly know a lot about this" (not in a sarcastic way).

- Appeal to the rest of the group by saying, "Come on, don't let Peter do all the work."

- Give the person a role to play which allows them to use their knowledge, e.g. leading a group activity or working with someone who knows less than they do in a coaching role.

- Don't say to someone, "You seem to know a lot about this, would you like to come up and run the session?" That may be exactly what they do want and they may take you up on your offer. Worse still, they may do a better job than you did.

The joker

- Focus on any serious point they make rather than the "joke", smile but then probe them further on the point with a straight face to indicate that you want to move on

- Set an appropriate tone yourself. If you've previously encouraged a very relaxed atmosphere and made amusing remarks yourself (which is generally to be encouraged) you may have given this person the impression that "anything goes". Reassert yourself by changing the tone for a while and making the discussion a little more focused and serious.

- Don't get involved in banter with the participant or try to be wittier or quicker than them, this will only encourage them and you may end up in a "who can be funnier?" contest which will distract from the purpose of your training.

- Give the person a role to play, perhaps in leading a review, where they can "perform" with your permission so that they get the attention they may want without causing disruption.

The challenger

- If someone challenges what you say, be prepared to back it up with evidence but don't let it turn into a protracted debate about the rights or wrongs of your position.

- Open up the discussion to the rest of the group and find out their opinions (without asking them to choose sides between you and the participant). This will give you a chance to see whether anyone else feels the same way as this person.

- If necessary, end the discussion by saying, "Well, we'll just have to agree to differ about this. Let's move on now."

- As with the other examples, find a moment to speak to the person in a break and ask for their support in helping you keep the course moving along. You could flatter them a little by saying you find their comments interesting and you'd love to have a really good debate about some of the points but point out that you do need to get through the material so that everyone gets something from the course.

Chapter 11: How To Evaluate Training

Why evaluate training?

Once you've finished a training course, you may just feel like slumping in a chair with a bottle of something and putting your feet up.

Alternatively, you may be on a "training high" and feel like running round the block a few times to burn off the energy. It gets us all in different ways.

What you probably won't feel like is carrying out a thorough evaluation of the training you have just delivered. But that's what you need to do, in some form.

After all, you and the participants have just invested a certain amount of time in the event, you need to know whether that time was well spent or wasted. In particular, you need to know:

- Did the training achieve its objectives?

- Did people learn what they were supposed to learn?

- Was the investment of time and money worthwhile?

- Has the training made a difference to people's performance?

- Was the training well – designed or do changes need to be made?

- Was the training well – delivered?

- Was it pitched at the right level, delivered to the right people?

Who needs to see the results of any evaluation?

That depends on the level and the type of feedback received, but it may include:

- the trainers involved in designing and delivering the course

- others in a training or HR department

- the people who sponsored the course (i.e. paid for it or authorised it)

- senior management in an organisation

- line managers of the people on the course

In some organisations, evaluation of training is very limited. It's generally assumed that training must make a difference but there's often little attempt to gather reliable evidence to support this. One reason, as I'll explain shortly, is that there are some real practical problems in gathering the evidence needed.

Some trainers may feel a certain reluctance to ask for feedback after a course, after all no-one likes to open themselves up to potential criticism, but any professional trainer will accept that it's part of the job. Few other people ask for, and receive, such immediate and direct feedback on their performance as trainers.

And, of course, it's not a bad thing. If there are criticisms of the course or the delivery, it's best to know about it so that you can improve and develop (and, if you're not interested in that, why are you involved in training?). Who wants to be running a course which isn't achieving what it's supposed to?

And, if the feedback is very positive, you can use it to support what you've done.

This is very important in some organisations where training is seen as an expense rather than an investment, something which can be cut if times are hard and where those involved in training may need to have as much evidence as they can get to justify their existence.

It's also important, of course, if you're an external trainer and you need to justify the fees you've charged for running the course.

Levels of evaluation

The most common form of evaluation is the feedback sheet given out at the end of the course. However, this only measures one level of feedback, an immediate response from the participants.

In the 1950s, Dr. Donald Kirkpatrick developed a model for evaluating training which included 4 levels.

This model remains very useful and relevant and is still used by many people as a guide for evaluating training.

Level I - Reaction

What did the participants think of the training?

This is what's measured by the feedback forms handed out at the end, the so-called "happy sheets" which often ask questions about:

- the content of the course – whether anything else should have been included or something left out

- the level it was pitched at

- the delivery skills of the trainers

- what the participants will do differently following the course

These forms are sometimes dismissed because they may just reflect how the participants feel at the end. And they do have their limitations:

- They tend to measure an emotional response, if people enjoyed the course, they'll tend to give it higher marks

- If they found the course very challenging or dull, or if they received some critical feedback, some participants will mark the course down

- Often these forms are handed out right at the end and participants don't feel like taking the time to complete them thoughtfully

- The participants may not know what else could or should have been included in the course

- The participants haven't had much time to reflect before giving their feedback

However, even given their limitations, these forms can still give very useful information about the design and delivery of the training. They're certainly much better than nothing.

There are different ways to measure people's reactions.

Numbers

On a scale of 1 – 5, where 1 = poor, 3 = good and 5 = excellent, please rate the following:

The trainer   1 2 3 4 5
The content 1 2 3 4 5

Words

Which of the following words would you use to describe the training?

Exciting Stimulating Interactive Dull

Scale of agreement

On a scale of 1 – 4, where 1 = Disagree strongly, 2 = Disagree, 3 = Agree and 4 = Agree Strongly, please mark the following statements:

The course achieved its objectives 1 2 3 4
The trainer was well prepared   1 2 3 4

Open questions

Which sessions did you find most useful and why?

How could the course be improved?

A numerical approach helps you to collate the answers in a statistical form, e.g. it can tell you that the venue averaged 4.2 or the trainer averaged 4.8, but it doesn't always help you to learn why.

To find out more about people's reactions, you need to give them space for comments and/or ask open questions. These can't be collated as easily as numbers but they give you more valuable information.

How to get a response

Make sure you allow enough time for people to complete the forms. Ideally, don't leave them until the very last thing before everyone leaves or you'll find a lot of empty space where the comments are supposed to be.

Give out the forms before the end and stress that you really value people's comments. Tell them how useful their feedback will be and how you'll use it.

Put some time into setting up the evaluation, as you would any other activity. I've seen trainers hand these out and virtually say, "Well, it's the end of the course, but we've got to fill these in before we go. Can you just leave them on the table on your way out?"

What about sending forms to people after the course so they have time to reflect before filling them in?

This sounds like a good idea. However, in practice, it doesn't always work so well.

The advantage of giving out forms on the course itself is that you have a captive audience and the return rate tends to be 100%. If you allow people to take forms away with them, or send them out after the course, you immediately hit problems with getting them back. People have other things to do after a course and filling in the forms becomes a very low priority.

Of course, you don't have to wait until the end of a course to get a response from participants. You can find out what they think as you go along, perhaps after each session or each day if it is a long course.

If you want an immediate guide to how people are feeling, just ask them! Chat to them during breaks and get a feel for how the course is going.

You can ask things like, "Is the course covering the areas you need to it cover? Is this what you were expecting? Can you see how you can put these ideas into practice?"

Or get them to write comments on a flipchart or on Post–It notes which they leave behind at a break.

Level II – Learning

At this level, you get feedback on how well people learned what they were meant to learn.

You should refer back to the objectives set for the training and see whether these were met. Of course, it helps if you set some and if they were specific and measurable, otherwise it won't be very easy.

The training will have been intended to have an impact on people's knowledge, skills and/or attitudes. How do you check whether it has had this impact?

Some ways in which you could measure what people have learned are:

- written tests – paper or computer – based

- practical demonstrations, e.g. of how to use some equipment or software

- case studies

- simulations or role plays to demonstrate skills

- self – assessment

- questionnaires

- interviews

- "on the job" observation by colleagues or trainers

- feedback forms completed by colleagues and/or clients

Whichever method you use, you'll need to test before and after the training. If you don't test beforehand, how do you know how much progress the person has made?

This level of evaluation raises some potential problems, which is one reason why, as I mentioned earlier, many forms of evaluation stop at the first level:

- Testing before and after an event takes time

- If you decide to use a written test, designing an accurate, standardised test also takes time and may require particular skills – it's easier to use such a test to check certain technical knowledge than to test for skills or attitudes

- If you use some other form of check, such as observation or feedback from colleagues, this involves numerous other people and needs their support and commitment. They need to understand what you're looking for and what the purpose of the exercise is

- Many of these methods have some subjective element, which makes standardisation difficult.

However, although these are real problems, they're not insurmountable and they don't negate the benefits of having this level of evaluation. As with the "happy sheets", the fact that the system may not be perfect doesn't mean that it has no value. You just need to be aware of some of the limitations of any approach you use.

Level III - Behaviour

This level of evaluation determines to what extent the learning has been transferred back to the workplace or applied outside the training room.

This could be argued to be the most important level since, if the learning has had no impact on someone's behaviour, what was the point? Indeed, some would say that, if a person's behaviour hasn't changed, then no learning has occurred.

There's a bit of an overlap with Level II here in that you're checking whether there's evidence that learning has taken place. The difference is that this is more about whether people are *applying* the learning.

Where Level II testing would take place immediately after the course, perhaps before people leave, Level III testing will take place over a given period following the course.

Methods for assessing this are similar to Level II and could include:

- interviews with participants and colleagues

- focus group discussions

- observation or supervision

- questionnaires

- feedback forms from colleagues and clients

Of course, this level has its own challenges.

First of all, will the participants have an opportunity to demonstrate their new behaviour after the course?

Often people are sent on courses to learn new skills but then aren't given a chance to apply them for some time afterwards.

You sometimes hear the expression "just in time training". What this means is training which people receive at just the right time so that they can put it into practice immediately. Unfortunately, it doesn't always happen.

I've run a number of skills courses where people were sent along who had no immediate plans to implement the skills I was helping them develop. For example, people on Train the Trainer courses who weren't going to be involved in any training for months after the course.

Will the workplace support the new behaviour? This can't be taken for granted. In some organisations, people are trained in new approaches but the culture hasn't changed to keep up. In other words, people around them may still be using "old" methods and may actively discourage them from adopting the new approaches when they come back from the training.

This is the, "You don't want to do it like that. This is how we do it around here" problem.

Are the necessary resources in place to allow people to apply their new behaviour? I remember being on a course myself once where I was shown how to use some new software, but then didn't get it on my computer until a few weeks later, by which time I'd pretty well forgotten everything.

How long after the course will you check the behaviour and over what period? How long will it take to establish that the behaviour is being demonstrated and that it will continue?

If someone's behaviour does change in a given period after training, how can you tell how much of that is down to the training itself rather than to other factors, e.g. just having more experience in the job?

Again, these problems should not prevent evaluation taking place. In fact, the process may highlight areas which need to be addressed.

For example, if there are resource problems, these need to be identified. If there are prevailing attitudes which prevent people putting new approaches into practice, these need to be tackled, perhaps through further training. Or maybe there needs to be more discussion at senior levels within the organisation to help bring about a change in the culture.

Level IV – Results

Here you're measuring the business impact of the training – are the benefits worth the investment?

If you're responsible for a training budget, how can you demonstrate that you're spending it wisely? How can you justify asking for more resources or holding on to the resources you've got? Why shouldn't the business just close down the training department and save the money?

Harsh questions, but ones I have heard in real meetings where people were making real decisions about funding.

What difference does your training make to the profitability of the business?

You may be helping people to learn new information, to develop new skills or attitudes. You can demonstrate that the learning is effective and the new behaviour is being applied in the workplace. But what difference does it actually make?

For many trainers, and training or HR departments, this is one of the hardest questions to answer. And in some organisations it's never asked. There's just an assumption that training must be "a good thing" (which, of course, it often is).

But, in many businesses, that only applies when things are going well. If times are hard, and people start looking at budgets and areas for saving money, it becomes a major issue.

To establish the impact of training, you need to go back to:

- the learning needs which were identified which gave rise to the training

- the objectives for the training

Why did people need the training in the first place? What business case was there for setting up the course? What was the need which gave rise to it? What was the problem which the training was meant to solve?

If the groundwork was done before the training was commissioned, then it should be quite clear how to measure the impact of the training. Depending on the subject matter, the benefits of the training may be, for example:

- increased sales

- reduced turnover of staff

- reduced absenteeism

- increased productivity (which can be measured in various ways)

- savings in time taken to complete tasks

- higher quality of goods produced, less waste

- people passing professional exams in less time and with fewer failures or re-sits, saving time and expense

- people being able to use new equipment, saving time and increasing productivity

In some cases, a monetary value can be placed on the impact of the training, which can be shown as the ROI (Return On Investment).

Some things lend themselves better than others to this sort of evaluation. If the aim is to change people's attitudes, e.g. on a diversity course, what will be the measurable impact on the business? It's a bit harder to establish in that case than if you've been training people to use a new software package.

When to use these levels of evaluation

I'm not suggesting that you need to use all four levels of evaluation every time you run a course. Which ones you use will depend on who needs to see the results and why you're evaluating.

For example, you may need to use all four levels to evaluate a new course which costs a lot of money to set up or which involves a lot of people. Once the course has been shown to be effective and worthwhile, it may not be necessary to carry on evaluating all four levels for every event afterwards.

Similarly, if you run a one – off event for a small group of people which doesn't involve a huge expense, it may not be cost – effective to set up an elaborate evaluation process to follow it.

Think about evaluation right from the start. If you identify a training need, think about how you'll test whether that need has been met and what impact this will have.

When you write your objectives, consider how you'll measure whether they've been achieved. You may also need to gather resources and support to help you carry out the process once the training is over.

Tempting as it may be to just switch off after a course, congratulate yourself for a job well done and head for home, there's still work to be done. Whichever form of evaluation you use, the work hasn't finished when the course is over.

What Will You Do Next?

In this book you have all the information you need to become an outstanding trainer. How are you going to use it?

However many ideas you've picked up from reading this, none will be of any use to you if they stay inside your head. Do something with them.

You should have quite a list of learning points and actions to take. Pick a few and make a commitment to try them out.

Some may be fairly simple to put into effect, such as making your training room more attractive or sending out pre – course information. Others may involve developing new skills which will require practice and may take some time.

Use the book again and again to keep adding to your toolkit of techniques and ideas, keep coming back to it when you want more tips or when you need a refresher. Keep it to hand when you're training so you can dip into it if certain situations arise (for example, if you encounter some "difficult behaviour").

And keep watching other trainers and learning from them. Be on the lookout for good practice. Watch people with very different styles to yourself and see what you can pick up from them, often the people you learn most from are those who come at things from an angle you would never have thought of.

Above all, have fun! If you don't enjoy it, the people you're training won't either.

Bonus Materials: There are some free bonus materials available to supplement what you have learned here, including examples of:

- an evaluation form

- pre-course materials and questionnaire

- post-course follow-up materials

To access your bonus materials, go to:

www.transformyourtraining.com/book-bonuses

And, if you haven't already, make sure you sign up for my **Training Tips newsletter** so you receive regular articles to help you develop even more.

Just visit the website at www.transformyourtraining.com and sign up for the free report on the Home page.

You can also follow me on Twitter at
www.Twitter.com/AlanMatthews11
and get my daily training tips and general observations.

Good luck and best wishes.

Alan Matthews

Appendix 1

Resources you may need for a training session

Here is a list of possible resources for a training session. You may not need all of these but it is a reminder of some key items and a few suggestions for others you may not have thought about. Some of these things you will take with you, some may be provided at the venue.

If you expect anything to be provided, check that this is the case and find out who is going to set things up for you. Get their name and contact details. Arrange to meet them well before the start of the training to make sure everything is set up as you want it.

- flipchart stands and plenty of paper

- prepared flipchart pad with your own visuals ready to use

- laptop and projector if needed

- if you use someone else's laptop, make sure you have their password

- external speakers for laptop if using sound

- extension leads

- PowerPoint slides on memory stick or on computer

- interactive whiteboard if needed

- TV or monitor if needed

- DVD player if needed

- video equipment if needed, including power leads and connectors

- camera to take photos of participants

- USB memory stick with any slides you plan to use

- any workbooks to be used

- any handouts to be use

- evaluation forms

- CD player, iPod docking station or other source for any music you're using

- plenty of A4 paper

- pens for participants to take notes with

- lots of flipchart pens and/or whiteboard pens

- pieces of coloured card to write on and stick on flipchart or hang from line

- a washing line (or string) and pegs to hang cards from

- medals and trophies to use as team prizes

- fiddle toys such as springs, bendy people, pipe cleaners

- bright buckets or other containers for flipchart pens

- A4 cards with your own images on or laminated posters

- glue and magazines for making collages with pictures

- multi coloured paper and card

- Koosh balls (soft fluffy balls to throw around)

- mini notebooks

- lots of Post-it stickers

- BluTack

- blank playing cards

- name cards and/or badges or blank labels

- coloured lining paper to cover tables with

- masking tape

- Sellotape

- scissors

- certificates for participants

- sweets, chocolates and/or dried fruit for participants (and you)

- stopwatch, clock or other timer

- bells, whistles or other noise makers

Appendix 2

10 things to send people before a course

Your aim should be to get your participants excited and interested before they arrive for the training. Here are some suggestions for things you could send them.

1. An outline of the course (with an interesting name) showing the key topics to be covered, stressing what they will learn and the benefits they will get from it.

2. Information about yourself, including a picture, contact details, background about who you are and some information which makes you sound like a friendly, approachable yet professional human being.

3. A puzzle or brain teaser related to the topic to make them curious.

4. Some questions about the topic to make them think and to get their interest.

5. A link to a webpage with a video or audio clip about the training or the topic.

6. A cartoon which relates to the topic.

7. All relevant logistical information, e.g. venue, date, timing, parking arrangements, travel.

8. A list of who will be attending so they know who else will be there.

9. A brief questionnaire to find out more about them and what they need to get from the training to make it worthwhile.

10. A short task related to the training to connect it to their real working lives, e.g. a time journal or a few questions to ask people they work with.

There are two key things here:

1. Don't give people too much to do or it will seem onerous and put them off. So choose one or two from questionnaires, tasks, etc. Don't ask them to do everything.

2. Make all your materials and information colourful, bright and interesting so they will assume that the training itself will be like that as well.

Bonus materials: Don't forget to claim your free bonuses, including examples of pre-course materials, by going to:

www.transformyourtraining.com/book-bonuses

How Can I Help You?

I work with organisations to help them build outstanding training teams and to ensure that their training programmes are well designed, well delivered and effective.

I can do that by:

- running an in - house Train the Trainer course, from a 1 day workshop to a comprehensive 3 or 4 day programme

- working with your training teams to review your training materials and helping to redesign them or finding new ways to make them more lively and engaging or

- starting from scratch and doing some simple training needs analysis or evaluation of your current training to see where it might need some changes

You'll find details of the services I offer on the website at www.transformyourtraining.com.

All my training courses are interactive, entertaining and fun but they also give you very practical tips on how to design and deliver effective and engaging training sessions. Whether you're a beginner or an experienced trainer, you'll take away new ideas to transform your training.

I'm happy to come in and talk to your training team or your HR department to discuss ways in which we might work together. Please feel free to pass my name on to anyone you think might be interested and ask them to give me a call.

Alan Matthews

01564 770436

www.TransformYourTraining.com

References

The Learning Cycle And Learning Styles

D.A. Kolb (1984) Experiential Learning: experience as the source of learning and development New Jersey: Prentice-Hall

P. Honey & A. Mumford (1982) Manual of Learning Styles London: P. Honey

R. Dunn & K. Dunn (1978) Teaching students through their individual learning styles Reston, VA: Reston

Evaluating Training

D. Kirkpatrick *Evaluating Training Programs: The Four Levels* San Francisco: Berrett - Koehler

Memory and The Brain

H. Ebbinghaus (1885/1962) Memory: A Contribution To Experimental Psychology New York:Dover

J. Medina (2009) Brain Rules Pear Press

R. Winston (2003) The Human Mind Bantam Books

R. Carter (1998) Mapping The Mind Phoenix

A. Curran (2008) The Little Book Of Big Stuff About The Brain Crown House
D. Gamo & A. D. Bragdon (1999) Learn Faster And Remember More Geddes & Grosset

Who Is Alan Matthews?

I'm a trainer, coach and speaker based in Solihull, West Midlands and I run a business called Transform Your Training.

I work with organisations to help them build outstanding training teams. I help trainers build the skills and confidence they need to convert whatever content they're dealing with (however dry or complex) into exciting and engaging training.

I've been involved in learning and development for over 20 years.

I've been running Train the Trainer courses for over 18 years, helping hundreds of people to become outstanding trainers.

I've run my own training business since 2003. Before that, I worked for Deloitte, one of the top professional services firms. I was initially a Tax Consultant but moved into training. I wrote and delivered both highly technical courses (if you want a challenge, try and make Tax interesting!) and skills courses – Presentation Skills, Train the Trainer, Management and Leadership, Client Service, Networking Skills and many others.

So I know exactly what you need to deliver effective training, whether dealing with complex technical information or "soft skills".

Many years ago I was a Primary Teacher and taught English As A Second Language to 4 and 5 year olds. (I also worked for the Inland Revenue for a while, but I don't like to talk about that).

I'm available to run training courses or to speak to conferences or meetings. Visit the website at www.TransformYourTraining.com for more details.

You can also download free articles and reports from the website and join my mailing list to receive my regular **Training Tips newsletter**.

6575682R00172

Printed in Germany
by Amazon Distribution
GmbH, Leipzig